Praise for Here's My Card . . .

"Rare is the book that leaves my forehead so sore. *Here's My Card* made me smack my skull with the palm of my hand at least once on every page. Over and over, I thought, 'Of course! That's a great idea; how come nobody (including me) does that?' No book I've ever encountered will produce more business results per invested dollar or minute than this one. Every technique is cheap, fast, and easy . . . and each will surely produce huge returns. Best of all, every page is fun to read. Everything about *Here's My Card* is a real joy!"

>—George Walther
>Speaker Hall of Fame member and author of
>*Phone Power, Power Talking,* and *Upside-Down Marketing*

"Bob Popyk has turned a simple business card into a multi-faceted marketing tool. After reading *Here's My Card,* you'll certainly stop and think of the opportunities which abound next time you hand someone your card. Great material for every sales and marketing professional!"

>—Dennis M. Houlihan
>president, Roland Corporation U.S.

"I wish I'd had this book years ago. It's so packed with client-attracting nuggets of ideas that I'm giving it away to my clients."

>—Kare Anderson
>Emmy award–winning journalist and author of
>*Walk Your Talk Cross Promotions*

"*Here's My Card* is so full of information, it's hard to imagine ANYONE not learning something significant and new from it. Bob proves why he's a guru of low-cost m⸍ ' ⸍- ing and PR. He does more with a simple business card than m⸍⸍ whole campaign—and his insights are refresh⸍⸍ about business cards, it's about changing your mote yourself and your business! It's absolute

>—Randy Beck
>director of professi⸍
>NAMM-Internationaᵣ ₘusic Products Association

"In this age of ever-increasing over-connected technology, it's absolutely amazing how this book can bring you back to basics, using something as simple as business cards to find more business with a minimum of effort and stress. We're recommending this to our entire dealer network."

—Tom Riggle
senior manager, Honda Marine
American Honda Motor Co., Inc.

"Entertaining, practical, clever, creative, and especially BELIEVABLE advice for increasing business through business card networking. Here is more of the Popyk magic at its best!"

—Bob Moffit
vice president, Kawasaki Motors Corp.

"Here's a compilation of great easy-to-use networking ideas that will absolutely work. If you have business cards, you need this book!"

—Brian Majeski
publisher, *Music Trades Magazine*

"This is great writing with a great message. Most business people I know don't know how important something as simple as a business card is if used properly. Everyone in business should read this book."

—John Spitz
director of education
National Kitchen & Bath Association

"Bob cleverly shows us all how to use our business cards as one of our most important networking tools! Thanks Bob. Great stuff!"

—Thomas J. Winninger, CSP, CPAE
author of the bestsellers *Price Wars, Sell Easy,* and *Full Price!*

Here's My Card

How to Network Using Your Business Card to Actually Create More Business

BOB POPYK

RENAISSANCE BOOKS
Los Angeles

This book is dedicated to all those in today's business world who realize it's not "who you know" but "who knows you" that makes the major difference when creating more clients, customers, and sales.

Library of Congress Catalog Card Number: 00-100888
ISBN: 1-58063-113-4

10 9 8 7 6 5 4 3 2 1

Design by James Tran

Published by Renaissance Books
Distributed by St. Martin's Press
Manufactured in the United States of America
First Edition

ACKNOWLEDGMENTS

Thanks to all the readers of my columns who sent in business cards and networking ideas to be used in this book. Also, special thanks go out to those who heard me speak at conventions or dealer meetings and took the time to share their thoughts on what works and what doesn't when exchanging business cards.

I appreciate the help of Ian Culver, editor at Renaissance Books in L.A., and Joe McNeely at Renaissance in New York who liked the idea of this book from the very beginning, the help of my literary agent Sheree Bykofsky who really excels at her job, and thanks to my friend Michael Schwager at Media Relations who came up with the title.

A deserved round of applause should go to my editorial staff at Bentley-Hall, Inc., including Michelle Brunton, Kristin Johnson, Danielle Norman, Honore Berger and Antoinette Follett. Thanks for their help in getting this book to press. They are easy to work with.

Acknowledgement and sincere thanks also goes to all our clients and the industry associations who gave their support for this book. I learned there are no bad ideas. Some are just better than others. And the better ones are inside this book.

CONTENTS

Foreword   17

Introduction   20

PART I
Networking Know-How and Business-Card Savvy

CHAPTER 1   Who Was That Masked Man?   25
Leaving an Indelible Impression

CHAPTER 2   The Power of Positive Linking   26
Capitalizing on Your Own "Magic Circle"

CHAPTER 3   Take Me, I'm Yours   29
It's All About Presentation and Delivery

CHAPTER 4   Watch Your Mouth   30
Things You Should Never Say When Handing Out Your Business Cards

CHAPTER 5   R-E-S-P-E-C-T   35
A Few Tips for Properly Giving and Accepting Business Cards

CHAPTER 6   Compliment Your Way to Success   36
Sincere Compliments Can Make All the Difference When Handing Out a Business Card

CHAPTER 7   Staple This . . .   39
Sending Business Cards in the Mail

CHAPTER 8   The Keys to the Palace   41
Making a Lasting Impression with a Receptionist or Secretary

CHAPTER 9   . . . And One More for the Road   44
Tips for Giving Out an Extra Card

CHAPTER 10   Can I Have a Double?   46
When to Ask for an Extra Card

CHAPTER 11   Use Your Own Business-Card Code   47
Quick Ways to Sort Out Your Cards on the Run

CHAPTER 12   Don't Trust Your Memory   48
Keeping Track of the Business Cards You've Given Out

CHAPTER 13   Bulletin-Board Bonanzas   50
Bulletin Boards and Business Cards

CHAPTER 14   Sowing and Reaping and Sowing Again   52
Whatever Happened to . . . ?

CHAPTER 15   Read Once, Speak Twice   53
What's That Name Again?

CHAPTER 16   Can I Have It Back?   55
A Tough Approach to a Hard Sell

CHAPTER 17   If the Phone Doesn't Ring . . .   58
Handling People Who Take Your Business Card but Won't Return Your Calls

CHAPTER 18   How Many, How Much, How Often?   60
Ideas for Determining How Many Cards to Have Made

CHAPTER 19   My Dog Ate My Card; Got One of Yours?   61
What to Do When You're Down to Your Last Card

CHAPTER 20   Would You Feel Comfortable
              Giving Your Card to . . .   63
Using Your Personality to Overcome Your Card's Imperfection

CHAPTER 21   Giving a Card to Mr. Know-It-All   65
Exchanging Cards with Less-than-Amiable People

CHAPTER 22   Give a Card . . . Lose a Sale   68
When Not to Use a Business Card

CHAPTER 23   On a Scale of One to Ten   71
Rating the Meeting or Exchange

CHAPTER 24   Mr. or Ms. Customer, C'mon Down!   72
Ten Ways to Get a Response

CHAPTER 25   Business Cards and Referrals   74
How to Get Referral After Referral

CHAPTER 26   Thank You, Thank You, Thank You!   77
Thank You Notes/Business Cards

CHAPTER 27   Follow That Truck!   80
Investigating the Competition

CHAPTER 28   Do It to Me One More Time   82
How Many Times Do You Give Your Card to the Same Person?

CHAPTER 29   Call Me at Home . . . Any Time   84
Using Your Home Phone Number to Your Best Advantage

CHAPTER 30   Goofy Is As Goofy Does   86
Two Stories about What Not to Do

CHAPTER 31   Overcoming the Fear of Trying   88
Confidence Problems and Presentation

CHAPTER 32   You've Got to Have a Plan   90
Expanding Your Magic Circle

PART II
Personalized Presentations

CHAPTER 33   Let the Games Begin   94
Clever Quotes and Notes

CHAPTER 34   A Perfect Match   97
Presentation: Paper Clips, Gift Boxes, and Ribbon

CHAPTER 35   Star Search   99
Stars and Other Stickers

CHAPTER 36   Personalization at Its Best   100
Signatures, Titles, and Other Personalizing Touches

CHAPTER 37   Cool As You Want to Be   102
Silly Titles and Silly Cards

CHAPTER 38   Bounce-Back Business   104
Business Card Coupons and Freebies

CHAPTER 39   Money Talks   106
Using Money with Business Cards

CHAPTER 40   Hey, You Never Know   108
Lottery Tickets

CHAPTER 41   You May Have Already Won . . .   109
Your Own Little Contest

CHAPTER 42   You Have Already Won!   111
Assorted Freebies to Get Attention

CHAPTER 43   Richard, Dick, Richie, or Rich?   112
Nicknames on Cards

CHAPTER 44   I Forgot My Cards   113
Examples of Business Card Substitutes

CHAPTER 45   14-Karat Customers   115
Two Set Trick—One Set New, One Set Old

CHAPTER 46   Is That the Phone?   116
Ringing Telephone Card Holders

CHAPTER 47   Highlighting for a Real Impression   118
Highlighting, Circling, and Calling Attention to Specifics

CHAPTER 48   Keep on Clipping   119
Clipping Articles to Put with Your Cards

CHAPTER 49   Gotcha!   120
Catching Someone's Attention

CHAPTER 50   The W. C. Fields Approach to Business Cards   122
Being Persistent

CHAPTER 51   Stupidity Seldom Works   124
A Time and Place for Comedy

CHAPTER 52   I'll Send It to You   125
Getting Someone's Home Address Can Be Revealing

CHAPTER 53   My Card, My Job, My Resume   127
Resume Cards

CHAPTER 54   Rubber Stamps and Business Cards   129
The Flexibility of Rubber Can't Be Beat

CHAPTER 55   Cards That Aren't Cards   131
Giving Gifts or Premiums Instead of Cards

✓ CHAPTER 56   Keep It Clean   134
Business Card Cases

CHAPTER 57   When You're Smiling   135
Presentation Cleverness

CHAPTER 58   It's Not Brain Surgery,
              It's Not Rocket Science . . . It's Common Sense   137
A Little Recap

PART III

Creative Design . . . It's All in the Cards

CHAPTER 59   How Much Is Too Much?   141
What Information a Card Needs

CHAPTER 60   Both Sides Now   144
Two Sides or One?

CHAPTER 61   Creative Ideas for the Back of Your Card   146
Relevant Information to Increase Your Card's Value

CHAPTER 62   Sometimes Less Is More   150
Simplicity in Layout Can Be Good

CHAPTER 63   A Perfect Angle   151
Using Different Shapes

CHAPTER 64   Rolodex™ Perplexed?   153
Rolodex-Ready Cards

CHAPTER 65   Ten Things You Never Want to
See on a Business Card   155
They Aren't As Obvious As You Think

CHAPTER 66   Skip This If You're Not Photogenic   158
Photo Cards

CHAPTER 67   Beam Me Up, Scottie   161
Holograms

CHAPTER 68   Plastics   163
Plastic Cards

CHAPTER 69   The Sweet Taste of Success   164
Candy Cards

CHAPTER 70   Cute . . . Real Cute   167
Cartoons, Drawings, and Illustrations

CHAPTER 71   What's That Name Again?   169
Phonetic Spellings

CHAPTER 72   Konichi Wah   170
Foreign Languages

CHAPTER 73   Crayons and Calligraphy   173
All I Need to Know I Learned in Preschool

CHAPTER 74   X Marks the Spot   175
Maps on Cards

CHAPTER 75   Here's Looking at You, Kid   177
Mirrors on Cards

CHAPTER 76   Pennsylvania 6-5000   179
Updating Changes

CHAPTER 77   I Love a Mystery   181
Clarity and Explanation

CHAPTER 78   Pop-up Pop-ups   183
Pop-up Cards

CHAPTER 79   Double Duty   185
Cards That Serve a Practical Purpose: Magnets, Slide Charts, Bookmarks

CHAPTER 80   First a Quarter, Now a Nickel   187
Leaving Room—Minimalism

CHAPTER 81   Don't Be a Victim of Hype   188
Avoiding Exaggeration and Falsification

CHAPTER 82   Born in the USA   190
Drawing on National Pride

CHAPTER 83   Everybody Loves a Winner   191
Awards and Accomplishments

CHAPTER 84   Bullets and Borders   193
A Little Creativity Goes a Long Way

CHAPTER 85   Leather and Metal and Everything Else   195
Your Card Doesn't Have to Be Paper

CHAPTER 86   Sniff Here   197
Scratch 'n' Sniff Cards

CHAPTER 87   Big, Bigger, Biggest   198
Oversized Cards

CHAPTER 88   Which Type Is Right for You?   201
Different Fonts and Type Sizes

CHAPTER 89   Green Means Go   203
Color Choices and Combinations

CHAPTER 90   Hold Me, Fold Me   206
Folding Your Business Card

CHAPTER 91   Check Out the Competition   208
Taking Cues from Other Business Cards

CHAPTER 92   The Internet and Business Cards   210
Web Addresses

CHAPTER 93   Feel Me, I'm Embossed   211
Embossing

CHAPTER 94   Signs of the Times   212
Look at Billboards for Inspiration

CHAPTER 95   The Best of the Best   214
The Best Cards to Go to for Examples

CHAPTER 96   In Conclusion   218
Things You May Not Have Considered

CHAPTER 97   Postscript   220
You'll Never Believe This One

FOREWORD

How many business cards have you given out over the years? How many have you received? Hundreds? Thousands? Tens of thousands? How many of those people do you stay in touch with on a regular basis? You can probably count them on your fingers. The rest were the people who were happy to give you their card during a few magic moments when your lives crossed. And then they were gone. Vanished. Never heard from again. Maybe you did business with them. Maybe you didn't. Maybe there was a business relationship. There was a reason, even if it was fleeting. Now if all of those people who gave you all of those cards don't call, don't write, or don't contact you in any way, think of the enormous opportunity you have if you contact them. You do the networking. You do the schmoozing. You develop and maintain your own platinum pipeline. You control your own golden database that could result in a lifetime supply of business. Business cards are a start. Personal linking is what makes things happen. If there's no follow-through, nothing happens. That's what this book is really about.

Back up for a minute. In this world of people and businesses things have changed over the years. In the past, someone spoke to you while they looked at you, and you talked back. That was personal communication. Today, impersonal communication pervades. Face time is less. E-mail is more. Handwritten notes and letters are going the way of the rotary-dial phone. Today we have voice mail, electronic junk mail, fax mail, pagers, beepers, palm pilots, digitized greeting cards, and digital cellular phones.

Business cards are the wave of the future, as well as the way of the past. We had business cards yesterday, and we have business cards today. And we'll still be using business cards tomorrow, no matter how highly technologically advanced we get. They are not going away. Business cards stand out. They are still the non-computerized networking wonder in today's digital world. They are personal, gracious, and mark you as someone of world class. They are not, and never will be, out of style. Business cards can differentiate you and make you unique in your own way. Craig Wilson, staff reporter for *USA Today* says, "You know the Latin: Cardnito ergo sum!" (Roughly translated it means "I have a card, therefore I am!") It's great that you have a card, but business cards by themselves do nothing. It's the person behind the card, and how they maintain the connection that makes the difference.

Think about it this way: In business, first you build your lifeboat, then you build your yacht. Your lifeboat is all the people you come in contact with over a period of time. Your yacht comes from keeping in touch with all those people on a regular basis. You start building your lifeboat through exchanging business cards. On the days when your yacht starts to sink a little, you can always go back to your lifeboat. The customer rapport you develop through keeping in touch makes sailing much smoother.

Business cards are "people linkers." They are used for networking, schmoozing, connecting, reaching out, prospecting, selling, and basic advertising. They can help you find a customer, make a sale, get a referral, increase your social life, and create your own personal PR. Knowing how to use them creatively and cleverly is one thing. Wanting to do it is another. This book will help you with the first. You're on your own when it comes to doing the second.

"Networking" (and all the other synonyms connected with this sometimes overused word) is what propels anyone in business. Without constantly expanding your horizons with new contacts—contacts which develop into new customers—sales and revenue can start to slide. There are reasons why people fall short when it comes to networking. For example, studies confirm that 70 percent of salespeople fail in their first year because of the fear and apprehension associated with prospecting and networking . . . getting out and finding people to talk to. Anxiety and fear are productivity busters. Overcoming this apprehension can be as easy as coming up with ideas to make something as simple as a business card work in getting over the personal resistance barrier. Businesses fail for the same reason. Businesses, professional services, and salespeople start to get into a slump because they are not reaching the right people, or they're not finding more people to sell, service, or administer to. They fall short because they don't work their contact list, they don't expand their pipeline, they don't stay in touch creatively and systematically. "People-linking" is part of the answer. Business cards are part of the process. "People-linking" worked a hundred years ago. It still works today.

So intelligent, creative, consistent networking is the secret. Staying in touch is the answer. Constant contact makes the difference. It starts by using your business card to set yourself apart from everyone else at the moment, and use your "people-linking" skills to stay ahead of the pack for a long time afterward.

INTRODUCTION

You've got a job. You've got a business. You've got business cards. They all go together. You also probably have a phone, a fax, and a computer. Those are things we continually upgrade, and we always make sure they're working every day. But sometimes it's not quite the same with business cards. No upgrades. No checking to see if they're working. Sometimes we give them out to anyone who wants one, and sometimes to people who don't care either way. We give them out, that is, if we remember to keep them in easy reach. And many times we take them for granted. You know, "Here's a card, call me when you're ready." "Here's my card, keep me in mind." It's kind of like saying "have a nice day." It comes out of our mouths. Whether we mean it, or whether it gets heard, is another story.

But business cards can be one of the most effective ways for finding new business, creating more business, and leaving a lasting impression. Those little billboards with your name on them that you keep in your purse, in your pocket, or in your desk drawer can help you make more sales, create more customers, and increase your business overall. You just need to use them with a little cleverness and creativity, and you have to use them the right way. You need a plan, you need a specific goal, and you need to be creative. You also need something unique.

Millions of business cards change hands each day, yet very few actually create more business, make more sales, or produce more customers. Take a look at your own business card right now. Is it a great commercial for you and your business or service, or is it merely a piece of paper with a name, address, and phone number? Business cards are an incredible tool for actually creating more business because:

1. They're incredibly cheap to print.

2. You can give them out like crazy.

3. You can be as creative as you want to be with them.

4. You can have as many versions as you think necessary.

5. You can update them and change them as often as necessary.

But, no matter how great your business cards, if you keep them in your desk drawer, at home, or in your pocket, they aren't helping you create more business. They do you no good unless you get them out in circulation.

This book is about getting them out there. It's about getting them in the hands of the right people. Using them to your best advantage. Networking. Schmoozing. And being clever about it.

Remember how Vince Lombardi, the great coach of the Green Bay Packers, used to start his first practice session at the start of each new season? No matter how long the players had already been with the team, his first words on the first day of practice were, "Gentlemen, this is a football!" He never wanted his players to take anything for granted. It was always back to basics.

There are some real basics to remember when using business cards:

1. You need to have them with you at all times.

2. You have to get people to read and retain them.

3. You want to hand out something that's a great reflection of you and your business.

4. It's the person behind the card that makes all the difference.

Exchanging or handing out business cards has become one of the most common forms of introduction, surpassed only by the handshake. If your business card makes the first impression, then shouldn't it make a *great* impression? Otherwise you can just write your name and phone number on the back of a napkin and leave it at that. You might save a few bucks that way, but you could be losing a lot of new business, as well as a lot of repeat business. Could your card or technique be better? It's your call.

handy 3-inch ruler

1   2   3

GARY GREENBERG
Comedian • Writer
(212) 677-3821

fold here to
use as toothpick

to childproof,
cut along line

NETWORKING KNOW-HOW AND BUSINESS-CARD SAVVY

Take a look at your business card now! The first part of this book contains ideas for using your business card to create more business. That's assuming you have a great business card already. The last part is how to make your business card look more effective. So, if you don't already have a creative, clever, interesting, well-thought-out business card, skip ahead to the back of the book. And after you create a business card you can be proud of . . . something that people will keep and show to others, then you are ready for new creative ideas for finding prospects, creating customers, and increasing your profits.

WHO WAS THAT MASKED MAN?

Leaving an Indelible Impression

Think of the Lone Ranger. With a flurry of hooves, a cloud of dust, and a hearty "Hi-yo, Silver," the Lone Ranger rides off into the sunset. "Who was that masked man?" everyone wonders. And what did he leave behind for the people? A shotgun shell? A spent .22-caliber cartridge? No. A silver bullet! Something that set him apart from all the heroes of yesteryear. So, you've got two choices when handing out your business card. You can hand out a silver bullet in a memorable way, or you can just take a spent shell out of your pocket and hope for the best.

A business card is your signature. It reveals a lot about you. The Lone Ranger didn't carry his silver bullets around in his pocket, getting dirty, scratched, and dusty. He kept them in his ammo belt so they always looked brand new. And he always presented a silver bullet in a way that made the recipients proud to accept it. They were happy to receive it. They didn't throw it out. They kept it around. They couldn't wait to show it to their friends.

So don't leave a potential customer saying "Who was that masked man?" Think about that the next time you say, "Here's my card!" Make sure they not only know who you are, and what you do, but most important, leave an indelible impression so they keep you in mind for the future.

THE POWER OF POSITIVE LINKING

Capitalizing on Your Own "Magic Circle"

You need more than a good-looking business card to help create more business for you. What's even more important is the person behind the business card. A jerk with a great looking business card is still a jerk. You need a little personality along with personal contact. You need to work on your schmoozing skills, and you need to capitalize on your own "magic circle" of influence. The more people you talk to, the better your chance of doing more business. Business cards are an integral part of networking.

When someone asks what you do, you have the perfect opportunity to give out a business card. You explain what you do as you hand over your card. Harvey MacKay, best selling author, suggests the multiple-choice response to the question, because it gives the other person more than one possible way to connect. He says that his typical answer is something like this:

"One, I sell envelopes. Two, I write self-help books. And three, I jog. I'm always looking for ideas for one and two, and trying to figure out how to get paid for number three."

Do you have a unique answer when someone asks what you do? What do you say when you hand out your business card? Come up with something that fits your personality, something that can make an impression. Then all you have to do is start finding more people who you can give your card to.

Maybe the next person doesn't necessarily need your product or service. Maybe they're not interested in your type of business. But once you establish a little rapport, get them to be your friend, and after you find out what they do, you might just say "If you were to go into my business tomorrow, who would you talk to?"

And most times you get a name. Much of the time it will probably be to get you off their back. But hey, you might just get a great lead. A super contact. Someone else to give your business card to.

So who do you know? Who can you know? Here's a little checklist of people you can give your business cards to, people who might be able to use your product or service, or might be able to put you in touch with somebody that can.

Where do you look for more prospects and customers when there's no one left to talk to? Everyone has his or her own circle of influence. These are the people you go to, not just for business, but for referrals as well. Keep in touch with these people on a regular basis to increase your day-to-day traffic. Write down your circle of influence.

- Who do you know from your old job? from school or college? through your kids? because you rent or own your home?

- Who do you play golf with?

- Who do you hunt or fish with?

- Who has sold you suits? a car? your glasses?

• Who did you receive a letter from today?

• Who did you write checks to this year?

• Who owns a hardware store? a grocery store? a shoe store? a furniture store? a dry cleaners? a new home? a business that's booming?

• Who is your barber/hairdresser? your jeweler? your dentist? your florist? a new neighbor? in your lodge or club? your painter or decorator? on your Christmas list? an architect? your physician? a realtor? your lawyer?

• Who manages or runs a movie theater? your bank? the local fitness club?

• Who was at your wedding?

• Who took your latest family photos?

• Who sings in a church choir?

The function of your business card is a simple: to let people know who you are, what you do, and where to contact you.

3

TAKE ME, I'M YOURS

It's All About Presentation and Delivery

Wouldn't it be nice if your client or customer couldn't wait to get your card? You're doing the talking, and they've got their hand out, almost begging for your card. Far-fetched? There are ways to do it. One way is to not give your card to your client or customer the moment they request it. Hold it in your hand first. Tell them what's important on the card. Handle it carefully, as if it were crystal. Start to give it, hold it back for a second, then say something like "this is important, keep it in a safe place," or "this will save you money, hang on to it." "Are you absolutely sure you want this?" "I really value who I give these to."

Stress the value of having your phone number handy. Elaborate on the benefit of a business relationship with you and your company.

What you're really doing is reciting a ten-second commercial for you and your business while handing out your card. Be creative. Get it down to where you know exactly what you're going to say as you give someone your card. Write it down. Look at it. Change it. Make it better.

What you say at the time you hand out your business card can have a lasting impact. Practice it. Come up with something that fits your personality. Try it out on your family and friends. See what works for you.

4

WATCH YOUR MOUTH

Things You Should Never Say When Handing Out Your Business Cards

You hand out your card. You want to say something at the same time besides, "here ya go." What you say sets up the tone of their impression of you. Here are ten things that should *not* come out of your mouth when you hand over your card:

1. Shoot, this is the only one I've got . . . must've had it in my pocket when I had my suit cleaned.

2. Never mind the stuff I've written on the back. It was too much to erase.

3. Sorry it's bent, gotta get some more printed up.

4. This is one of my co-worker's cards. Mine are coming soon. Let me just write my name on it.

5. Excuse the dirt, it must've fallen out of my case.

6. This is from my last job, but my home number's the same.

7. Could I have it back? There's a phone number I need on it.

8. Whatta ya think of my business card? I spent a ton to have them printed. Feel the raised printing.

9. Our company likes to spend a lot of money on our business cards. They should spend less and pay me more.

10. My cell phone number, home phone, Web site, e-mail address and fax number are not on the card. Here, I'll write them down on the card for you. Oops, I need more room. Got a piece of paper?

You also don't want to use swear words. I remember going into a car dealership and looking at a new vehicle that seemed rather pricey but that had piqued my interest. When I asked the salesperson for his card, he said "Oh s**t, they never give us enough of those damn things. What the hell do they expect me to do . . . Hold on . . . I'll write my name on this piece of scrap paper . . . Hope you don't mind." It didn't really entice me to spend upwards of 40K with him or his dealership.

Remember George Carlin's "seven words you can't use on television?" When giving out your business card, those seven words are only a start. There are many words, phrases, topics and discussions you can't get into unless you want to run the risk of really irritating someone . . . to the point where they won't do business with you regardless of the price of your product or service.

Here are some guidelines on words and phrases you should be aware of when giving out your card. If you're the type of person that likes to "shoot from the hip," these are some of the things you should avoid:

• four-letter words or anything you can't use on the airwaves

• sexual innuendo

- discussions relating to sex or sexual preferences

- religious convictions

- political views

- ethnic backgrounds

- opinions on multi-level marketing programs

- self-praise

- making fun of someone's musical tastes

- anything controversial like the Ku Klux Klan, Mike Tyson, O. J. Simpson, or Jimmy Swaggart

Think I'm kidding? If a customer starts using expletives in the course of conversation while exchanging cards, should you try to be his buddy and start using them back? I'd watch it. Better you should bring the customer up to your level, rather than let him drag you down to his. Remember the saying "familiarity breeds contempt?" Think about it next time you want to join in with your best Andrew Dice Clay dialogue. Save it for the local bar.

Don't even think about commenting on anything to do with marriage, sex, or alternative lifestyles. If a husband says "Give me your card. I'd like to buy it, but I want to discuss it with my wife first," don't come back with "What kind of wimp are you?" or "If she leaves because you bought it, you might luck out." These kinds of responses won't sell much. Friendliness, compassion, and common sense probably will.

If, in an effort to create rapport with your customer, the subject of Rush Limbaugh, the Bill Clinton presidency, or Don Imus comes up, I'd get out of the conversation quick. You don't know what side your customer is on, and he might be setting you up. A middle-of-the-road policy makes the most sense.

Stay away from anything argumentative, controversial, or stupid. I was in a store once when I overheard a customer say: "I'd like to have your card and think about it. By the way is that price $195 or $795?" The salesperson said, "What are you. . . . Polish?" He was. He left. I don't think he ever came back either.

You learn the hard way. I speak from personal experience. A few years ago, I wrote a column that appeared in many magazines about not telling people when business is bad. People love to spread rumors, and the people you tell that "things are slow" will then tell their friends, who tell their friends . . . and "it will soon be like a bad Amway convention." It was a joke . . . to everyone except the solid, dyed-in-the-wool Amway dealers who read the column. They sent letters to the editor, called me on the phone, and canceled subscriptions. I'm still sending letters of apology.

Think that everyone shares your musical tastes? Try making light of accordions or ethnic music. Most people make a little fun of polkas once in awhile. Miller beer tried it with a commercial in a hip and trendy bar, where a customer says he's going to put money in the jukebox to play a polka, and the whole bar goes quiet. Funny, huh? The thousands of letters and complaints they got from polka-lovers made them think otherwise. They pulled it after the first time out.

Something else. Pull back on self-praise when handing out your card. "We're the biggest, the best, the greatest" worked for Muhammad Ali. But, it may cost you business if you overdo it. Humbling yourself with phrases like "I want to earn your business," and "I want to make sure you're happy," can run rings around your competition.

Be very aware of your customer's feelings and sensitive to their likes and dislikes when handing out your business card. Don't stereotype people into categories. Treat ethnic groups as friends rather than sales challenges. Be nice. Watch your mouth. Try a few random acts of kindness. Get to know your customers and clients better, but stay away from topics like the ones listed earlier. Find out where they live, their work, and their hobbies. Talk about books, movies, sports, or something related to your business. But don't go into the danger areas. Stay away from thin ice. Don't play with controversy. You want to create business and make a friend. When something controversial comes up, do a little side-step. Once you tick somebody off, it's very hard to get them to do business with you. Just keep one thing in mind . . . if it sounds unprofessional, it probably is. Choose your words carefully.

5

R-E-S-P-E-C-T

A Few Tips for Properly Giving and Accepting Business Cards

The Japanese have a neat way of exchanging business cards. They hold their card in front of them with both hands. It's almost a ceremony. They hand the card over with a slight bow. You're expected to do the same. They admire your card and comment on it. You do the same when receiving their card.

Don't take a person's card and not look at it. Don't immediately stick it in your pocket. Don't fold it in half. Don't pick your teeth with it. If you do, they might do the same with your card. You might turn their card over and jot down a note relevant to the conversation. That may encourage them to do the same with your card.

I love it when somebody says to me, "What a great looking card!" It makes me brighten up. You get what you give. Act accordingly when exchanging business cards. Treat someone's business card as you would like yours to be treated.

Also, don't shake hands and give out a card at the same time. When you shake hands, look at the other person. Acknowledge their name. Say something positive. Then when you exchange cards, make it special. Don't treat giving out a card as an afterthought.

"Do unto others as you would have them do unto you" works in life. It also works with business cards.

6

COMPLIMENT YOUR WAY TO SUCCESS

Sincere Compliments Can Make All the Difference
When Handing Out a Business Card

Ionce heard that the easiest way to get people to like you is to find
something that you truly like about them, then compliment them
on it. Sometimes it can be tough. Do you remember your mother
telling you, "If you can't say something nice about somebody, don't
say anything at all"? You can't sell anything to anybody by keeping your
mouth shut. Some salespeople never seem to get over this hurdle.
Others seem to excel at it.

One of the problems is that we never know what might offend
someone. I remember going into a Sears store to buy a CD player.
After looking at all the models on display, I had a question. The only
clerk I could find couldn't help me, so she called the office for assistance. The next thing I knew, there was a page yelling out, "Would
someone help the gray-haired man in stereos?" I bolted for the door.
Maybe I've got gray hair, but sometimes to me it's bleached brown. I
don't remember getting gray. Gray is for old people. I'm not old. Don't
remind me about it. Don't ask me if I want a card. I'm out of there.

Anytime a salesperson shows me an item and the price is too
high, I always say "Can I have a card?" That coupled with "I'll be
back" is an easy way to get out of there quick. A short time ago I
went to buy a golf shirt at Nordstrom's. Now, I can buy a golf shirt

from Penney's for $39. The Pro Shop at our club usually has $49 golf shirts on sale for $75. (Nike has to pay Tiger Woods somehow). So I guess I was prepared to spend up to sixty to seventy bucks or so. I went to the menswear department, took a shirt off the rack, and tried it on. When I came out of the dressing room to look at it in the big mirror, the clerk said that the shirt fit, but what did I think about the style? I didn't know. My daughter always tells me what's cool and what's not, and she wasn't with me. So I asked him, "What about the style?" He said it was a more mature look, and I seemed to be a younger guy. I liked this person already.

I asked him what he suggested, and he took me to a table with the new Calloway shirt line. He showed me a silk golf shirt. It had a lining and unique buttons. The pattern was outstanding. I went in to try it on, and when I came out, the clerk said: "Wow, that looks absolutely great on you. You could wear it to play golf or underneath a sport coat. You look like a golfer—being tall and thin. You probably have a lot of golf shirts, if you play all the time. You certainly look like you play the game." That's it. Sold.

I took out my credit card, had it rung up and then looked at the price. *A hundred and twenty dollars!* I thought to myself, "Am I crazy? A hundred and twenty bucks for a golf shirt?" Of course I didn't say it quite that way. Instead I said, "I could tell by the quality that it must be rather expensive." I signed the charge slip, smiled, and then very carefully carried it in the bag so it wouldn't get wrinkled. Inside the bag was a couple of the salesclerk's cards. He said "tell everybody where you got your shirt . . . I put a couple of cards inside your bag!" Now when I wear the shirt and somebody tells me how good it looks, I always say, "thanks . . . guess how much it cost?" I *love* to say, "It was a hundred and twenty bucks. Mike at Nordstrom's helped me select it. I have his card if you want see him."

If you exchange business cards with somebody with a bad attitude, it could be very tough to come up with a compliment. When all else fails, just smile. If they start being obnoxious, just keep smiling. Before long they'll want to know what you're smiling about, and they'll start smiling too. And then you can tell them they must be a very astute shopper, or they know your industry inside out, or just that they look nice. Maybe it's their clothes, their hair, their personality, their watch, or their car. Okay, okay. Maybe they have bad breath, green teeth, bratty kids, and questionable credit. Well, you can't just ignore them. You want them to be your friends. Find something about them you really like. Everybody has some redeeming qualities. At least that's what I've heard. Compliment them as you hand them your card. Compliment them when you ask them for their card. And you'll compliment your way into more business at the same time.

7

STAPLE THIS . . .

Sending Business Cards in the Mail

You have business cards. You get bills in the mail every day. You send out checks in the mail to pay these bills. Most retail stores, credit card companies, or utility companies supply you with an envelope. You pay for the stamp. Why not staple your business card right to the middle of the check you're sending in the mail? It's probably the most cost-effective advertising you're going to get. Here's the interesting part. Many times the same person handles your check month after month. They see your name and the name of your company along with what you do, month after month.

If you're a retail store, car salesperson, boat dealer, or insurance salesperson (the list goes on) they have to see your name even if it's just to throw the card away. Usually they have to get a staple puller to take your card off the check. If you're paying a bill to a local company or utility, it's even better. Now people are talking about you: "Here's that guy again." "Who's that?" "Charlie Myers from Stereos R Us." "He always staples his card to his check every month." It's word of mouth advertising and it costs practically nothing.

One word of caution: It's easy to staple your business card to a brochure, sales letter or any information you may be sending or handing out. But remember, it's harder to take it off and it leaves holes in both your card and the print piece. You might want to simply use a paper clip, or slip it inside.

Stapling and business cards are a one-sided convenience, and that's usually yours when handing them out. (The exception might be to a check.) If recipients want to staple your card to something, let them do it on their own. They can choose where it goes and to what. Think carefully before making that decision for them. Business cards have a life of their own. Your recipient usually decides how long that life is going to be. It's easier to remove a paper clip than a staple.

Another exception might be stapling a business card to an $8\frac{1}{2}$ x 11 blank sheet of paper when letterhead is not available. It could be a quote, a sketch, or information already on a plain sheet of paper. In this case you could staple (just once) your business card to the top center of the sheet of paper, pretty much where the name and address of your business would be if it were letterhead. Don't hit it twice with a staple. Once is enough, so someone can more easily take it off if they want to. It's easy to center with a staple rather than a movable paper clip, and looks a little better in this situation. You be the judge.

8

THE KEYS TO THE PALACE

Making a Lasting Impression with a Receptionist or Secretary

Many times you might use your business card to get past the gatekeeper—the receptionist guarding the door to your client or customer's office. Making a good impression with the front desk person can go a long way in getting you business.

Here are some tips when you don't know him or her, he or she doesn't know you, and you need to get an appointment or talk to a decision-maker:

1. Always be clear, concise, and to the point. Don't overwhelm him or her with details.

2. Never launch into your presentation. The receptionist doesn't really care.

3. Speak in a lower, slower tone of voice.

4. If the phones are ringing off the hook, don't start schmoozing and making casual conversation unless he or she initiates it.

5. Keep your radar alert at all times for ammunition—anything the receptionist/secretary says—that might be useful in dealing with the boss.

6. Be cordial and try to make a friend as quickly as possible, but keep it on a business level.

7. Earn his or her respect.

8. Respect his or her time.

There are some clever ways to present your card in a situation where the receptionist is overworked, strung out, and probably underpaid. You can stop at your local grocery store and pick up a small bunch of cut flowers from the in-store floral department (avoid romantic flowers like roses, etc.). Stapling your card to the stem of the flower can win you all kinds of points when you give him or her your card. Bet you get your appointment sooner and with a smile as well.

The flowers aren't necessarily a token of affection; you might have brought them just to dress up the office. Better still, you can do the same thing with packets of flower seeds. You don't have to worry about keeping them in water or having them look fresh. Everybody loves flower seeds, even if they never plant them. It's the thought that counts.

You can do the same by stapling your card to a recipe. Something that was "Mom's favorite." "Just want to pass it along to someone who might like to try it."

Premium items are also business cards. (For more on this, see chapter 55.) Anything that has your name, address, phone number, and company information on it serves the same purpose. So consider these items not for your client, but for the person who can help get you in to see your client, who forwards the calls, who can help get you in the door with a little rapport. Don't make the mistake of reserving that coffee mug, pen, pencil holder, flashlight, or whatever type of doodad just for the check signer. Pave your way in with the receptionist, switchboard operator, or front office person as well.

Premium items do, however, work with the client. And they work better if they are creative and a little out of the ordinary. I remember asking somebody for their business card, and they gave me a little gadget that opens the packaging on new CDs easily printed with their name, address, and phone number. You know how you want to open a new CD immediately after you buy it, as soon as you get in the car? It's great. I keep it in my glove compartment and see their name every time I use it. It's really handy. I even called them the other day and asked if I could have another one . . . and I found myself placing an order for their product at the same time. I probably wouldn't have called if their number wasn't right there in plain sight. Gadgets, gizmos, and doodads with your name on them have their place if you use them correctly.

9

. . . AND ONE MORE FOR THE ROAD

Tips for Giving Out an Extra Card

Most people hand out one business card at a time. Sure, they hand them out to as many people as possible, but I've found only a handful of people make a practice of handing out more than one at a time.

Of course you want to make sure your customer or client reads and keeps your card. But when they ask for your card, you might want to think if it could be a wise move to give them an extra . . . one to give to someone else. It depends on how well you know them, and the type of rapport you've established. Once you've gotten into the habit, enlisting the help of your customers to build your business is one of the easiest and most successful sales tools you can use.

But just don't hand someone two and expect that they'll get the hint to give one away. Ask them if they'd give one to someone they know to further whatever it is you do or sell. And also, don't give them more than two. Three or more diminish the value of the cards.

It goes beyond saying, "take two, they're small." Make sure your clients, fans, customers, and friends have another one of your cards to pass along, to give to someone else who could represent future business.

You want to make your recipients raving fans. A happy customer is a customer who is going to tell his or her family and friends about you and your business. Make it easy for your customers to refer other people to you.

It's also a great way to build your own active referral network. Give your customers an extra reason to send you new prospects. When you give out extra cards, write the customer's name on the back of each one. Explain that for every certain number of referrals, the customer is entitled to a free service or exceptional discount.

I know a New York hairstylist, for instance, who gives a free haircut to every client who refers three new clients to him. This particular hairdresser is in a hard-to-find location and does very little advertising. Yet his client base just grows and grows, and it starts with giving each client a bunch of cards to pass along.

Think about getting extra cards printed up the next time you're ready to order your new supply. You're not giving them away by the pound. You're not handing them out by the dozen. But if you hand someone your card like it has perceived value, then one more could be appreciated and it might be passed along. It's just common sense if you do it right. If you get one back, you've probably done it wrong. Test the waters. See what works for you.

CAN I HAVE A DOUBLE?

When to Ask for an Extra Card

It's one thing to give out two cards. It's another thing to ask for a second card. When someone gives you a card, always ask for another one for a friend, customer, whatever. When you give them your card, they might just ask for a second one as well. If they don't, they'll still think of your gesture as courteous, kind, and considerate. It could go along with establishing rapport, and making sure the recipient of your card puts it in their memory bank as received from someone who has their best interests in mind.

Don't just ask for a second card. Search your brain for a minute and think of someone who could use that person's card. Who can you refer them to? You want them to do the same for you, and there's nothing like a little honesty when you say, "Could I have another one of your cards? I might know somebody who I could pass this along to." Be sincere. Remember that you get what you give.

This is on the spot networking squared. You give out a card. You get one in return. The whole scenario is taken to a higher level by simply asking for a second card from the person you're exchanging cards with first. Tell them why you want it. Don't make it up. You never know where your next customer or client is coming from, and it could be the friend of the person right in front of you.

USE YOUR OWN BUSINESS-CARD CODE

Quick Ways to Sort Out Your Cards on the Run

Here's a great idea. You work a trade show, consumer event, Chamber of Commerce meeting, anywhere where you give out a lot of business cards. You also get a lot of business cards. It's easier to follow up contacts if you have a system that helps you remember what to do with them. Try folding down the corners of a card in such a way that it tells you whether to call them, write them, send them information, give them pricing, or whatever applies to your type of business.

For example, folding down the left corner could mean, "call them." Folding down the right corner could mean "send them your brochures, press kit, catalog, whatever." A bottom corner could mean, "don't bother." The other bottom corner could mean, "see back of card for more info." Set up a system that works for you and is easy to use with your business.

The idea is to get used to doing this. After a few times it starts to become second nature. Do it tactfully. Don't let the person think you are bending it over to throw it away. When you get a lot of business cards at one time, your own little system of bending the corners could save you a lot of exasperation when you review them the next day.

DON'T TRUST YOUR MEMORY

Keeping Track of the Business Cards You've Given Out

If you're working a trade show, a dealer meeting, or a business function with a lot of people, the cards start being handed out like beer at a clambake. Problem is, when we get a card from someone, after giving one of our own, we might not look at it again for several hours, or even several days. We may not be quite sure of the conversation that took place at the time. So when you're handing out cards, exchanging cards, or collecting cards, keep your own cards in a separate pocket or separate section of your purse. In fact, always have a suit or jacket with several pockets. Keep the cards other people give you in a separate pocket, or a specific part of your purse or briefcase. Always write on the card you receive in exchange, even if it's right during the conversation. And make sure you don't mix it with your own cards.

This is crucial if you've received a card from somebody who is really interested in what you sell, what you do, or what service you provide. In fact, if your client or customer sees you write the words "This is important!" on his card, he or she will probably feel really good about it.

Set up your own "one-person" filing system. One pocket could be for your own cards, another pocket for really hot leads and prospects, and another pocket for people who you will get back to in several days or weeks.

When you get back to your office or base of business, you can take out the cards in order of importance. See what you've got. The hot ones from your "hot pocket" get attended to first. The cards in the "whenever" pocket come out last, if they come out at all. They could even go right into the wastebasket if that's your decision. Saves time. Saves effort. And the best leads, prospects, or past customers can get to the top of the pile for immediate follow-up.

If you're using your business cards on a regular basis, it's tough to remember everyone you gave or sent them to. How many cards did you order the last time you had them printed? 500? 1,000? 2,000? How many do you have left? Where did they go? Strange, isn't it? One week you have a lot, the next week you have just a few left.

Donn Young, a registered Piano Technician in Devon, Pennsylvania, likes to keep track of who gets his cards. He left one card on a community bulletin board in the lobby of a local bank. A woman took the card and made an appointment to get her piano tuned. She then passed the card along to someone else who did the same. Approximately ten years later the trail led to over $42,000 worth of business from one card, and will continue to grow. Not bad for an investment of about a nickel.

If you find yourself giving out business cards to people who you think might be quickly discarding them, you might start to think twice about handing them out carte blanche. Don't worry about it. Don't give it a second thought. Buy more cards. Get them out there. Find more people to give them to. It's a numbers game. Those cards you hand out might not turn into business tomorrow or next week. But a month or a year from now . . . you never know.

13

BULLETIN-BOARD BONANZAS

Bulletin Boards and Business Cards

I didn't think I would ever take a business card off a bulletin board. That was until a few weeks ago. A friend of mine who owns a local bar put a business card bulletin board up near the juke box. And before you knew it, dozens of local business and services who were regular customers started putting their cards up. He supplied the classy colored pushpins. It was always kept neat. As I casually glanced at some of the cards, the ones with pictures immediately caught my eye first. And then I noticed the four-color cards with clever art. One limo service with a picture of their limos fanned four cards and pinned them to the board. It was the only business that put more than one card up. I took one of the cards. A few days later a client came into town. Rather than picking them up at the airport myself, I sent a limo for them. I used the limo service on the business card I saved from the local pub. Hey, you never know. Maybe those boards do work sometimes.

Business card bulletin boards are commonly found in public facilities and supermarket entrance ways. But if you want to get your name out in this way by using your business cards without spending a dime, don't forget about colleges, libraries, churches, hospitals, union halls, convenience stores, smaller shopping malls, social clubs, banks, factories, hospitals, restaurants, and bars.

These bulletin boards are a zero-cost source of sales leads for small businesses such as craft shops, professional services, trades people, and home-based businesses. They also work well with primary services such as auto repair, lawn care, home improvement, and cleaning services. These boards can be ideal for people who provide personal care services and in-home care products.

You need to go back and check the board once in awhile. See if someone has taken your card or covered up your card with one of their own. Replace it if it's gone. Give yourself a better position if it's still there. Who knows . . . someone with an immediate need might just see it.

14

SOWING AND REAPING AND SOWING AGAIN

Whatever Happened to . . . ?

Okay. You've given out your card. Nothing has ever happened as a result. No response. Call the person you gave your card to, ask if they still have it, and tell them to bring the card back. You need it for a promotion you're doing. You're having a contest, promotion, or sale, involving the people who you've given out cards to in the past. If they come back with your card, you'll give them a brand new one . . . plus a lottery ticket. Or maybe a five dollar bill, movie ticket, discount certificate, or any one of a number of things you can come up with. If they've thrown your card away, tell them you'll send them a new one in the mail, and to then bring it in.

What you're going to find out is who has kept your cards and who hasn't. It will also tell you if your cards are working for you. Don't just let the cards go out into the world and hope for the best. If more business is important to you, talk to people who've received your card once more. Talk to them again face to face. Find out why they didn't do business with you, and what it is going to take to get money out of their pocket, their signature on a check, or their name on an invoice or contract.

This is like Marketing 101, but on a very small level. It doesn't take much cash, and here's where your business card can generate some additional business you may not have planned on.

15

READ ONCE, SPEAK TWICE

What's That Name Again?

How often do you meet somebody, introduce yourself, hear their name, and then five minutes later, you have no idea what their name was?

When you receive someone's business card, here's a little trick that will help you memorize their name, and keep it in the back of your brain for a long time. When you get their card, comment on their card and say their name. You might ask if they know other people you know with the same name. Say their name out loud. Say it twice. Use it in conversation.

For example: They give you a card. You see their name. If you say it once, you'll remember it for a few minutes. Say it twice, and you'll remember it for days. If their name is Dave McAllister, you can say, "Dave McAllister . . . do you know the McAllister's in _____?" Or, "Dave McAllister . . . where does McAllister come from originally?"

Okay, that might sound a little weird to you, but it beats sneaking a look at the card again when you're halfway through the conversation and suddenly you can't remember their name. Or you call them by the wrong name.

If you're having lunch with several people who you have not met before, get their cards immediately, and then set them on the table next to your plate. Set them in the same order as the people sitting across or next to you, particularly if there are four or more. Do it discreetly. You can then sneak an occasional look to remember their names, titles, and positions. As you call them by name, and as you use their name in conversation, you can start putting the cards in your pocket.

Say their name. Repeat it twice. Use it in a sentence. Then put the card away. It's easy and it works.

16

CAN I HAVE IT BACK?

A Tough Approach to a Hard Sell

Michael Zapparo was trying to put together a deal with a major manufacturer looking to buy a sizable quantity of the product he was selling. The problem was that each time he had an appointment, there was somebody new in that department. Each time he was there, he left a card with the person, then came back the next time to find someone else in the chair.

About the fourth go-round, he found himself up against a new person whom he had little rapport with. After getting positive responses from the three earlier contacts, he gave the new person one of his cards. This person expressed little interest in him or his product. He was totally confused. So he just said, "Can I have my card back?" No explanation. Just asked for the card. So the new person gave him the card. Mike said nothing. The customer said nothing. As Mike put it, "We stared at each other for what seemed like ten minutes." Actually it was more like ten seconds.

In a situation like this, the first one who talks loses. And it wasn't Mike. Finally the customer, the new person in the driver's seat, said, "What feedback did you get from the other people here?" Mike said, "They loved the product and were set to order, then they got transferred. You don't like me or the product and I don't want to waste your time. By the way, they're not still with the company, are they?"

The customer then said, "Maybe I'll take a second look. Give me back your card and sit down for a second."

He got the sale. It started with asking for the card back. Sometimes you just have to have nerve when giving out (or taking back) your business card.

How about this? Is someone asking for your card because it's just a good way to get away from you? If people ask you for a business card too soon into a conversation, they might be looking for a quick way to escape. So if you feel this might be the case, and someone says, "May I have your card?" you could answer "Why?" And then, whatever they answer, you simply ask, "Why's that?" Do it two or three times you might be amazed at what you'll hear. It could go like this:

"May I have your card?"

"Why?"

"Uh . . . so I can have your name and address."

"Why's that?"

"So I can get in touch with you if I decide it's something I might need."

"Why's that?"

"Uh, well, we're just looking around right now, and don't even know if it's something we want to do."

(Then you can switch to the "Oh's.")

"Oh . . ." (pause)

"Yes we're really not in the market, but my sister suggested we stop by to look."

"Oh . . ."

"Yes, she's from out of state, and we're, like, killing time."

Kind of gets to the bottom line very quickly doesn't it? You can use "why," "why's that," "oh" or "and . . ." (meaning "what else are you trying to tell me?"). Try it once or twice to see if it works for you. It might save a lot of time, separate the suspects from the prospects, and move your business up a notch.

17

IF THE PHONE DOESN'T RING . . .

Handling People Who Take Your Business Card
but Won't Return Your Calls

W e've all been there. Someone expresses interest in our product or service, we give them a call and get voice mail. We leave messages. They never call back. We call them again. Nothing. No response. It happens all the time. So I will share a personal experience with you. This is absolutely true.

A few years back I met a gentleman at a business function who asked what our business was involved in. He asked for my card. He was vice president of marketing for a Fortune 100 company. He said he was interested in one of our programs and asked for a price quote. We talked for quite awhile and had a few laughs over drinks. A few days later I sent him a proposal based on what we had talked about. The price was in the tens of thousands and would renew every year. It was a big deal. I called him a few days after he got the quote and got his voice mail. I left a message and he never called me back. I left a couple more messages. Still nothing. I tried leaving funny messages, clever messages, straightforward messages. I checked with other people in his office to make sure he was not on vacation. He just wasn't returning my calls. I kept track of how many times I had called him over a three-week period. There were nineteen attempts. I called early morning, late afternoon, during lunch, in case he was still in the office, and any other odd time, hoping to catch him. Always voice mail. Never a return call. At that point I figured I didn't have anything to lose. He wasn't going to call me back, we didn't have a deal, so I decided to just give it one final shot.

I called at 2:00 P.M. the next day. But first, I called someone else in his department to make sure he was actually in the office. Of course, as usual, I got his voice mail. I said "Ron, this is Bob Popyk. I've called you about twenty times and left messages, and I'm not getting a return call. I'd like to get an answer on our proposal, even if it's just a no. At least I'd know where we stand and I'm starting to feel stupid. I checked directory assistance and got your home phone number, so if I don't hear back from you, I'll call you at home . . . at 11 o'clock this evening." I thought that would get his attention. No one wants to be called at 11:00 P.M., particularly if they go to bed early.

He didn't call back. I left the office and went home. 11:00 came around. I started thinking if you make a threat you should follow through with it. 11:05 P.M. My hands were starting to sweat. I had to call. 11:07 P.M. I dialed the phone. It rang. Ron answered. I said, "Ron, this is Bob Popyk." He said, "Where the hell you been? You said you'd call at 11:00. You're late." We got the deal.

I think there's a fine line between decent persistence and constant hounding. But when somebody takes your card, then doesn't take your phone call, you have lost nothing by being creative, clever, or assertive to try to get them to call you back. You don't need to bombard the person with messages, but try to find out why they're not returning your calls. Maybe it's your product, your service, your company, or you. Talk to other people in the organization to get some insight. Don't leave the same voice mail message each time, don't give up, and above all, use some personality.

18

HOW MANY, HOW MUCH, HOW OFTEN?

Ideas for Determining How Many Cards to Have Made

How many business cards should you order at a time, how much should you spend, and how often should you update or redesign them? Let's do the math. Here's a simple formula:

Take the number of cards you give out on average in a week and multiply that by fifty-two. Let's say it's an average of ten per week. Ten multiplied by fifty-two is 520.

Most businesses have at least four major trade shows or conventions a year. Figure on giving out between fifty and one hundred cards at any self-respecting convention. For our purposes we'll go with seventy-five. Four conventions times seventy-five cards apiece gives us a grand total of 300 cards for special events. Add that to your yearly total—520 plus 300 equals 820.

Then add 20 percent (20 percent of 820 is 164) for mistakes and throwaways. Add that 20 percent to the last figure (820). Adding 164 to 820 makes 984, so ordering a thousand cards is a safe bet for a year, depending on what your average daily use is.

Remember, you probably want to do only a year at a time. Area codes are frequently changing, zip codes change, offices move. You don't have the same computer you started with years ago. Your business cards should be upgraded as well.

19

MY DOG ATE MY CARD; GOT ONE OF YOURS?

What to Do When You're Down to Your Last Card

We've all been there. You're down to your last card and you hesitate to give it out because it looks like it just came out of a waste basket. Here's an idea for turning it into a positive experience . . . one your client or customer will remember. The first thing is to not just hand it out and hope for the best. It might be a better idea to acknowledge the fact that you don't really have a card that would be presentable, and you would be embarrassed to give them your only card. Be apologetic. Be sincere. Ask them if you could have two of theirs, one to keep and the other to write your information on.

Tell them you'll send them a fresh card as soon as you get back to your office. And when you write your name and address on the back of their card, be sure and put a big X across the front of their card so they don't mistakenly give it out to somebody, thinking it's one of theirs. (It happens all the time.)

Now, a couple of things will happen. They will insist on taking your card, even if it is worn. At least you've had a chance to get to know them a little better, even if you've just chatted about the dirty card. It will put you in a better light, to make up for the tattered card. At least you'll have an explanation.

If they agree, however, to let you write on the back of one of theirs, and give you two, now you've got their card, their name, company information, and so on. You've also started a conversation and possibly developed a little rapport.

You still want to send them a new card after you get back to your base of business. In fact, you probably want send them two if you think they would pass one along. And don't forget the "thank you" note. It's an easy way to create a great impression . . . even if your business (based on your business card) wasn't that impressive at your initial meeting.

20

WOULD YOU FEEL COMFORTABLE
GIVING YOUR CARD TO . . . ?

Using Your Personality to Overcome Your Card's Imperfection

W hat would you do if the president of the United States asked you for your business card? Or the CEO of Microsoft? How about the Pope? The Queen? If you had one chance to personally hand your business card to someone of great prominence and influence, and wanted to make a really good impression, what would you want your card to look like?

Tough question. Something off your copier? Something made off your computer printer? Probably not. Something from the quick-print store down the street? Maybe something better?

If your business card is really bad, or maybe just not the greatest in the world, think carefully about giving it out. Better to make no impression than a bad impression. If you've got a bad card, make it better. If you've got a fairly good card, what do you have to do to get it to the "best" level? Then how about your presentation? Check over the words you say when you give out your card.

But if you're stuck with your card, if you can't change it, if it's one your company supplies, you might have to deal with it. You can use your personality to overcome it. There are two ways to do this:

1. A sincere handshake and smile when you give your card.

2. A few words that are not only a short commercial for you and your company, but show you're a warm, kind, friendly, trustworthy, caring human being. That's not too much to ask, is it?

Hand out your card with some tact, some personality, and some sincerity. People can see behind the card. Let people know you can be a friend. Let them know you appreciate meeting them. A business card can only do so much. You have to do the rest. How does your business card rate? And how about you? Are you complementing your card?

21

GIVING A CARD TO MR. KNOW-IT-ALL

Exchanging Cards with Less-than-Amiable People

We've all had them. They come in many forms. Male and female. Young and old. They not only know it all, their parents knew it all. They've had uncles and cousins who knew it all. Give them a card, but don't try to explain a new product to them. They've been there, done that. Don't tell them what a value that new model is. They know the manufacturer personally. They may have been consulted before it went to market. They can buy it direct at cost. Even less from a catalog. And they've heard there's a site on the Internet that's practically giving them away. They're professionals, they have a friend who's a professional, or they have a relative who gave them all the advice they need to buy one of your products. They want you to feel very lucky that they'll even look at your business card.

How do you handle these people when you give them your card? First, do you want to handle these people? Let's assume for a moment that sales are really important to you, and you want to sell to these people in spite of themselves. That will show them; teach them a thing or two. Your product going out the door with their money in your pocket.

But how? How do you handle the know-it-alls before they just tick you off completely? First of all, Mr. Know-It-All likes to hear some of the following particular words and phrases:

- Wow, I'm impressed.

- No kidding, really?

- I'd love to get your opinion on this.

- What would you do if you were me?

- I'd like to earn your business.

- Could I use you as a referral if you do business with us?

- Man, I wish I could do that.

- I'd appreciate your help on this.

- That (whatever) looks great on you.

- Can I get your advice on this?

- I'm sure anybody in town would love to get your business.

- I'll work with you on this.

You get the picture. Unfortunately you have to be nice. That's really hard when you want to give someone a slap on the side of the head as you hand them your card. But don't lose your cool. Find out what you and your customer have in common. Get them to laugh. Be their friend. Don't use words and phrases like:

- Then go someplace else.

- That company will be broke in a month.

- Here, let *me* show you how this works.

- If you buy it someplace else, don't look to us for service.

- I'll give you one price, and if you want it, fine, but I'm not going to haggle with you all day.

Know-it-alls don't like pressure. They can't stand it. And I'll share this with you: in spite of what you might think, know-it-alls do buy products and services somewhere, they will pay more than wholesale, and they will pay for anything if they think value exceeds price and the salesperson is their friend. It's a fact. It's usually just one of those two things that's a problem when Mr. Pain-in-the-Butt sticks your card in his pocket and sneers.

Dealing with Ms. and Mr. Know-It-All can be very trying. It can be tough. But if they're looking for whatever you sell or whatever service you provide, they're probably going to get it somewhere. If you've got the tolerance, the tenacity, the personality, and the staying power to hang in there while they do a number on your head, you might luck out. Your competition will probably send them packing, thinking they've just scored a victory by not having to deal with them. If you shift gears, tell them what they want to hear, and make them a friend, they might just end up as a regular customer after you give them your card.

22

GIVE A CARD . . . LOSE A SALE

When Not to Use a Business Card

I hate giving out a business card if I know the person is just trying to get away diplomatically and will never do business with me. They think they're being polite.

If you're involved with a company that deals in business-to-business services, or you sell high-ticket retail, you'll recognize this next scenario. Now remember, this is not for professional services like medical, legal, accounting, or the like. This is where giving a card is a part of the norm. It's an everyday practice. You spend a lot of time with a client or customer, and then they say something to the effect of "I'd like to think about it. I'll get back to you." And guess what happens? *They never get back to you!*

We've all been there. You wait, you write letters, you leave messages. They never get back to you. If every retail customer who said "I'll get back to you," actually came back, there would be a line stretching from three states over to the front door of your store or business. Okay. That might be a bit exaggerated. Maybe they do come back, call back, or buy from you next time around.

Many times the easiest way for a client or customer to get you out of their face is to say "Let me have your card . . . I'll get back to you." They save face. They let you off easy.

Sometimes you might not want to give a card.

I know a salesperson who is a master at not giving out a card if he thinks the sale is going nowhere. The client or customer asks for his card and he simply says "Uh-oh, I wish you hadn't said that. It seems that every time someone asks for my card they end up not buying. If you're really not interested, just tell me up front. I'll save a card, and I won't have to worry about hearing from you again. If I give you a card, will you seriously think about it and let me know one way or the other?"

Most people don't have the personality to pull this off. But he gets more than his share of business by not giving out a card once in awhile.

You might think they really want a card, and really want to think about it. Or are you just giving out a card so your client or customer can drift away gracefully?

There are only three good reasons for not using business cards. One case is the person who has such a powerful presence that everyone knows who he or she is. This notoriety only applies to just a handful of people. The second reason is if something else would work better . . . a catalog, brochure, or something more significant like a book. But the third reason is to maintain control. This way you can always say "Let me take your card and I'll send you mine with some very relevant information."

If you're so famous that everybody knows your name, you probably don't want most people knowing where to reach you, so maybe you don't need a card.

If you're a writer, your latest book will work as well as a business card, particularly if you hand-write your address and phone number in it and autograph it as well.

But if you want complete control, get the name and address of who asked for the card and send them the information on what they're looking at, along with a card. This works great for salespeople selling boats, cars, insurance, RV's, computers, or any other premium high-ticket retail item. If your brochure contains your name and phone number, skip the card and send them the print piece. Tell them it's coming. You'll call them after it arrives to answer other questions.

Lou Holtz, the former Notre Dame football coach, took a coaching assignment at the University of South Carolina. He became the hero of the town. Constant media attention, TV interviews, national press coverage. He didn't have time to have new cards printed in time for a speech he was giving at a corporate event a thousand miles away. So he just gave an autographed picture of himself to whoever wanted one. One of those people sent him a letter in an envelope that simply had his picture and the address of "Columbia, SC" on the envelope. No name, address, or zip code. He got it. That's high recognition. If you're not that famous even in your town, if your fame and notoriety do not precede you, stick a few more business cards in your pocket.

23

ON A SCALE OF ONE TO TEN

Rating the Meeting or Exchange

When you exchange business cards, you might want to rate the conversation, the possibilities of doing business, or how your meeting, conversation, or presentation went. Keep the card and rate the results on the back of the card on a scale from one to ten.

If you feel the meeting went extremely well, give it a nine or a ten. If it was nothing spectacular, give it a five or six. If it didn't go anywhere, give it a one or a two. Now, even a week later, you can look at the card and know exactly where this conversation or meeting stood at the time. You can put the card in your follow-up file, and update it each time you have another conversation. Grade it each time you have any kind of communication with the person. Then every time you look at it you know where you are on the "close to getting business" scale.

Don't wait too long after the meeting or conversation is over. You can forget quickly. Put the number on the same spot on each card, each time you give a rating. You'll know where to look, and if you number the card each time you talk to the person, you'll know if the chance of doing business is going up or down the scale.

If you're in the insurance, real estate, automobile, or high-ticket retail business, this could be an easy way to keep a handle on how well you're doing with each lead, prospect, and customer.

24

MR. OR MS. CUSTOMER, C'MON DOWN!

Ten Ways to Get a Response

It's one thing to give a business card, it's another thing to follow up with the person who has your card and get them to do business with you. Here are ten ways to get your client or customer to respond after giving out your card.

1. Send a postcard with the words "Trying to reach you, please give me a call." Then simply write your name and phone number.

2. Call them during the day when you might usually reach an answering machine. Leave a message that says, "Hi (name), this is (your name) down at (your business). I've got good news for you." Everyone likes to get good news. Most people will call back if you leave a phone number and a time to call. Of course, you better have good news. It could be a sale price, a new product or service, better terms, etc.

3. Send them a thank you note just for meeting with you. Then follow it up with a phone call.

4. Have a picture taken with the two of you together. Then send the picture to them in the mail with a note to remind them of the conversation you had.

5. Call them and tell them you have additional information that you forgot to mention at the time of your meeting. Would they like to make an appointment to stop down to see you again?

6. Call them and ask if you can send them more print material on whatever product or service they're interested in.

7. Send a small gift thanking them for the meeting, the presentation, or the demonstration.

8. If you see their name in the local paper or industry trade publication, cut it out and send it to them with the words, "Nice going! Thought you'd like an extra copy."

9. Find an article in a magazine or paper that might be relevant to their business, cut it out, attach another of your business cards to it, and send it to them.

10. Get some information they might be interested in personally, like their hometown, their alma mater, or their ethnic background. Call them and tell them you have it, and ask permission to send it to them. This gets you into a further conversation, helps to establish rapport, shows interest, and helps to create more business. It all starts with your business card.

25

BUSINESS CARDS AND REFERRALS

How to Get Referral After Referral

It's not just "who do you know?" It's "who can you know?" that increases business, sales, and revenue. Referrals can be gold. It's easier to use a previous customer's name, the name of a friend, or the name of a relative to "grease the skids" when looking for new business contacts. But make sure you know who the person is and how credible they are before you use them as a reference.

A few years ago we were trying to get into the pool and spa industry. I asked one of my friends who had some visibility in the association if he knew one of the major manufacturers. He said "Absolutely, use my name. I know the vice president of sales personally. I went to college with him. He's one of my buddies. I've worked for their parent company. They know me. Tell them I said to call."

I knew that one member of the board of the company was also on the board of the association, and that they were interested in a book for their dealers on following up leads. Not only did we have a shot at doing the book, it would spin off a great number of speaking engagements with the association itself, and give us a shot at writing for the major industry publication. But each time I called and used my friend's name, I was treated very coldly. I could never get an appointment. After six months of trying I finally got to make a presentation at their company headquarters. I went into their conference room, introduced myself to everybody, and brought my friend's name up again. Silence. I had no idea that he had bombed when he worked for the parent company, that they thought he was unethical, and that he had had an affair with the president's secretary. It couldn't get much worse. I couldn't tap-dance my way out of my predicament fast enough. It was six months before we actually worked with the company.

So the moral to the story is: Make sure you know your referral's standing with your customer or client before you use their name. It's like using the name of a person who just filed bankruptcy when you're going to a bank for a loan. You don't want to do it. You have to be careful.

But referrals, if used correctly, are a great source of new business. Here's how to ask some magic questions when giving out your business card.

1. If you were to go into my business tomorrow, who would you talk to as a possible customer?

2. Do you have any friends or relatives that would be happy owning a (your product goes here)? I'd appreciate it if you could refer me . . . this is how I earn my living.

3. Who else can I make as happy as you are?

4. Who's the first person who comes to mind that I could send my card to as well?

5. We're very selective with who we work with. Is there anyone you recommend we consider working with?

You not only want to give out cards, you want to get them in return. You want to build yourself that platinum pipeline. So when you receive a card back, immediately write the pertinent information about the meeting on the back of the card. This is basic. Then don't just put them in a drawer someplace. Add these people to your own personal database. It will be your pipeline to success. The more people you know and the more people who know you, are what will determine how successful you will be.

Sort the cards out by whatever fields will be important to you. They could be friends, manufacturers, retail stores, purchasing agents, or whatever type of business you're in. Every time you talk to or write to the person, list it on their card or keep it in a database. Keep it up to date. After a while your gold list of prospects, customers, and networking resources will become a platinum pipeline.

It's one thing to have a pipeline. It's another thing to do something with it. You want to purge that database at least four times a year. Send a first class letter to everyone on your list. See which ones come back. People move. People die. Keep your pipeline up to date. Sort alphabetically and send something to all the A's and B's one week, the C's and D's the next. It could be a thank you note, a holiday card, or a new product or service note. It could be a discount certificate, or just a "haven't seen you for a while" card. It doesn't matter. Staying in touch is what matters. You want to keep your pipeline platinum. And that starts with keeping it up to date.

26

THANK YOU, THANK YOU, THANK YOU!

Thank You Notes/Business Cards

Everybody likes getting thank you notes. Nobody really looks forward to sending them out. Sometimes it can be a real pain. Remember, there is no standard size for business cards. How about a business card that's postcard size with the words "thank you" already on it. How about in longhand, in your handwriting?

Then you have a card that can be mailed, with your name, company name, phone number, and all other information already on it, "thank you" already scripted in, and a place for a personal note. How much easier can it be? It looks sharp, it's easy to use, and few people will copy the idea.

Most major retailers don't send out thank you notes. And most hospitals, clinics, service companies, associations, manufacturers, and larger companies don't either. If you buy furniture from Sears, a TV from Best Buy, a car from a local dealer, a computer from CompUSA, or office furniture from Office Max, chances are you won't get a thank you note. And if you do, it's not because the company insisted upon it. It's probably because the salesperson had a few business smarts.

One great example of the power of a business card with a thank you note happened to me not too long ago. I received in the mail a handwritten note from a men's shop where I had recently purchased a new suit. It was from the gentleman who sold me the suit, telling me how much he appreciated my business and hoped I would come back again. I was surprised to get it, because the men's shop was very small, and not only did this person sell me the suit, he tailored it personally as well. Not only that, he spoke only broken English. The note ended with, "Since this is how I earn my living, I want to make sure you are very happy. Maybe you will tell other people about my shop and I can make them happy, too. I want to earn your business. Thank you very much." *Business* was spelled wrong.

I remembered thinking of all the places I had done business in the weeks and months before, and nobody sent me a thank you note. Nobody called to see if I was happy. Nobody said "I want to earn your business." But Tony the tailor did. Tony's men's shop is in a little town of 30,000 people. It's twenty-eight miles from my office.

I remembered that on the receipt for the suit, Tony had written "Thank you!" and signed his name. I guess he felt one thank you wasn't enough. He had to follow it up with a note and a business card as well. Since he probably can't spend a thousand dollars a month on newspaper advertising, or big bucks in the Yellow Pages, and has no TV or radio budget, he has to rely on referrals and current customers. Does it work? He said he wanted to "earn my business." He referred to me as "his friend."

Now here's where the story gets better. A few days after I received the card and thank you note, Tony called me and asked how I liked the suit. Then he told me he had been thinking about me that morning . . . he told me he got a new assortment of men's shirts in, with some very unique colors and styles. He had one that would go great with my suit, and would I like him to send it over to me UPS? Of course. No problem. Send it right away. Did I ever ask "how much?" Nope. I forgot to. It never occurred to me. And even though I could have probably found a similar shirt in a local department store for half the price, I called him and ordered a second one so I could have a spare. It's amazing how a thank you note with your business card can set you apart from your competitors.

Maybe you did say "thank you" to your last customer, or after your last big sale. But what if you sent the people you do business with a handwritten note saying that you appreciated their business? And mention since this is how you make your living, you'd also appreciate it if they mentioned your name and the name of your business to their friends?

Think about it. Maybe you can't send a thank you note to everyone. But if you spend some serious time with a customer who ends up spending a lot of money, and you get to know him or her by name, maybe it would be a good time to start with a second "thank you." A note to their home or office. A note that asks that they come back again . . . to see you personally. What if forty percent of those customers came back to see you within thirty days or referred you to their friends as well? That could increase your business substantially.

If you have a thank you note/business card that can be mailed without an envelope, not only are you beating everybody to the punch, you could be running rings around your competition.

Something else: You could simply take your business card and attach it to a small sheet of paper (not $8\frac{1}{2}$ x 11) and write your thank you that way. Write it longhand. Make it look personal. How you do it is not as important as getting it done.

27

FOLLOW THAT TRUCK!

Investigating the Competition

This is marketing with business cards in its most creative form. A little one-upmanship on your competition. You have business cards and want to get them into the right hands. Giving out business cards to the wrong people doesn't help your business much.

If you're a fledgling business, or if you're a new salesperson working for a growing business, you might want to know where your competitor is getting their business from. This is not for everybody. In fact, this is mostly for business-to-business companies, or manufacturer reps who service a local or regional area. If your competition's trucks are clearly marked (and most are) take a day and follow one or two of their trucks around. After they make a delivery, jot down the company name, what they do, and when the delivery was made. Find out as much as you can about the company, and then go in and call on them personally in the next day or two. But don't go in with six pounds of literature, brochures, and print material. Just go in with your business card. And a small notepad. Leave the card and ask some quick information relevant to buying decisions, previous purchases, and so on.

Let them know you'll be getting back to them with more information based on what you've found out. Find out if there's any interest. Give your card to the other people involved in the business. Everybody gets one. Everybody needs to know your name. Tell them what you do, what you'd like to accomplish, and get out of there without taking too long. You can take up more time next time back—after you research the information you acquired on your "cold call" to your competition's customer. They have your card. They'll know who you are when you call or come back.

28

DO IT TO ME ONE MORE TIME

How Many Times Do You Give Your Card to the Same Person?

Okay, you've given your card to a customer or potential customer several times over the year or years. When is too many cards too much? Or not enough? The answer is: there is no answer. All clients and customers are different.

But using business cards effectively can be a numbers game. The more times you give one of your business cards to a person, the better your chance of creating new or more business. At least most of the time. The reasoning is simple. People change jobs. They change businesses. Their buying habits change. Who they do business with changes. You give them a card (and it makes no difference what type of business or profession you're in), and their station in life could change, their economic status could change, their business could evolve into something entirely different. They could simply misplace your previous card, they could have thrown it away, or forgotten it all together.

Your best bet is this: Any time you have a contact with your customer, either in person or by mail, give or include a business card. If they say they've already got one, ask them to pass it along to somebody who might also be interested. (This is just basic common sense and bears repeating.)

It's like media advertising. Many people don't react the first time they see a TV commercial or hear a radio spot. They don't immediately respond to the first ad they see in the paper. But seeing the same advertising over and over again creates a picture in a person's brain that may trigger some response. And sometimes the more times they get your business card, see your name, your company name, and what you do, the more apt they are to do business with you.

"You'd like a card? How many would you like? Would it be okay if I gave you two?"

On the other hand, sometimes persistence can get you into trouble. Another problem can be giving the same person your card over and over again. Great if you want them to retain interest. Bad if there is no interest and might not ever be. Sometimes you have to know when to give it up. Too many cards can sometimes be as bad as no card. Try, try again. And then if you don't succeed . . .

29

CALL ME AT HOME . . . ANY TIME

Using Your Home Phone Number to Your Best Advantage

Everybody's business card has the phone number of their business on the front. A business without a phone number is obviously a sign of no business. But how about your home phone number? That's something else altogether. If you're a doctor, insurance agent, automobile salesperson, heck, any kind of salesperson, sometimes the last thing you want is to have somebody call you at home. Particularly at 10:00 at night or on weekends or holidays. But put yourself on the other side of the business card for a minute. How would you feel when making a major purchase or being treated for a major illness, and having the salesperson or doctor hand you their card (after writing their home phone number on the back) and say, "Call me at home if you can't get me at the office"? You'd probably feel you've found the best place to buy a car or picked the right doctor. Excellent customer service is the ultimate marketing tool.

Okay, it's not for everybody. But if setting yourself apart from your competition is important to you, you might want to consider a second line into your home; a line that's connected to a separate answering machine. You probably have a dedicated line for your computer modem anyway. You can use that, or have a special line installed. That way those calls that come in on weekends or holidays, at midnight or two in the morning, can be retrieved at your convenience. It makes the client, patient, or customer feel special, and you have the advantage of a unique personal touch—something your client or customer might not get elsewhere.

That special home phone number is a nice touch, and personally writing it on your business card can set you apart from everyone else in your business. Keep in mind though, you do have to return the calls. Maybe not immediately, but the next morning, the next day, or within a reasonable time. Otherwise, that home phone will have a reverse effect and people will go out of their way to avoid you. You want to have an image of accessibility if it's important for your business. And you also want that perception to have some reality.

30

GOOFY IS AS GOOFY DOES

Two Stories about What Not to Do

There's a story about a car salesman who buys cards by the tens of thousands. When he goes to a football game and someone scores a touchdown he throws several hundred cards up in the air in celebration. His business cards go flying everywhere. People wonder what's being showered down on them and see his business card. They see his name. It's a great anecdote. What you might not know is that during one NFL game the home team scored six touchdowns, and he tossed about 3,000 cards up in the air, all over his section. After the game, the stadium officials called him on the phone and invited him to return to the stadium to clean up his mess. They knew his name all right. And it wasn't in a very good light.

Another great story is about a stockbroker who would go through a tollbooth and check his rearview mirror before paying his toll. If the car behind him was an expensive Cadillac, Mercedes, Lexus, or other, he would pay his toll plus the toll of the car behind him. He would then instruct the toll collector to give the next car a business card when they asked who paid the toll. The stockbroker's business card had a handwritten note on the back reading: "If you think this is creative, wait till you see what I can do with your stock portfolio."

Creative. Clever. Did it work? Well, most people ended up throwing the card out a little further down the highway. More litter. And when the bridge and highway department people started cleaning up the cards that read "If you think this is creative . . ." Well, you can figure it out from there.

Cleverness is one thing, goofiness is another. Use your business cards with some common sense. If it's not becoming to you, don't do it.

31

OVERCOMING THE FEAR OF TRYING

Confidence Problems and Presentation

Exchanging business cards is not difficult. It's an easy thing to do. But sometimes we can get ourselves into a rut where it seems that we're giving out cards and not getting anything in return. The customer doesn't come back, doesn't call, doesn't return calls, doesn't give us an order, or starts folding our business card in half as they're walking away.

Don't start being reluctant to give out a card because you don't want to be "pushy," or because you feel it might be inappropriate at the time. Nobody ever said, "Get that business card away from me!" Besides, it gives the recipient something to do with their hands. And don't forget . . . "Here's another one, in case you want an extra for one of your friends."

But certain social situations or situations where you're unsure of yourself or the client or customer might be intimidating. Here are some pitfalls to avoid.

1. Make sure you have your ten-second commercial down pat. Don't stumble over your words. Know what you are going to say when you hand over your card.

2. You have two ears and one mouth. Use them in that proportion when giving out your card. Listen more than you

talk. Let your recipient tell you a little about him or herself. Don't go overboard telling everything you know all at once.

3. You get what you give. Say something nice about your recipient. People like to hear positive things about themselves.

4. Humble yourself. Nobody likes an overbearing business card giver.

5. Get your recipient to smile. Humor can work wonders in a business situation.

6. Get your recipient to talk about him or herself. A great conversationalist is one who talks to you about yourself.

7. Get your recipient to like you. If they like you, they will trust you. If they trust you, they are more apt to do business with you.

8. Show a genuine interest in the person you are giving your business card to.

9. Look your recipient in the eyes when giving your business card. The eyes are the windows to the soul.

10. Be yourself. Use your personality when giving out a business card.

32

YOU'VE GOT TO HAVE A PLAN

Expanding Your Magic Circle

Where's your next promotional, advertising, marketing, and one-on-one advertising campaign using your business cards coming from? Do you have any plans, or are you just going to wait for the next person to come up and ask you for your card, and hope for the best? How bad do you want to create more business with your business cards?

Maybe you have an extensive advertising and marketing budget, or maybe you have none at all. With business cards, "none at all" will work if you have an idea, a plan, and a desire to get the cards out there. Of course a creative, distinctive, and clever business card helps as well.

Here's a little game plan that will work: If you really want to create more business by using your business cards, start sending out or handing out a minimum of sixteen a day. Do it first thing in the day, or as soon as possible as time permits. The first four cards should be sent to people who you already do business with. Thank them for their business with just a small note. Hand-write it. Include your business card.

Then send out four cards to people who you would like to do business with, who you've already talked to and who aren't currently customers. Send them a note with your business card, letting them know something new about your business, product, or service that they weren't aware of before.

The next four cards should be names right out of your daily paper. People who made the news. (Let's assume it wasn't the obituaries or police reports.) Congratulate them on the press they received, clip out the item, and send it to them with your business card and a note saying "Nice going! Here's another copy of the article. Thought you'd like to have it."

Then give out at least four cards to people who might not be customers, prospects, or clients, someone who likes you, respects you, and who you have good rapport with. These people might know someone who could possibly help create more revenue for you. Just give them a card and ask "If you were to go into my business tomorrow, who do you know that I could pass my card along to?"

That's a minimum of sixteen cards a day, in just a few minutes of your time. Multiply that by five workdays in a week, and that equals eighty cards in a five-day period. Multiply that by 4.25 weeks in a month and that totals out to 340 cards to people who might do business with you, or could help increase your business. If just 25 percent of those cards generate more business, that's a significant amount of customer or client revenue from just a simple plan for getting your business cards out to the public.

Follow-through is important. Getting people to ask for your card, accept your card, look at your card, and keep your card is critical for actually creating more business. It's simple, it's cost-effective, and it sure beats keeping your business cards in the bottom left-hand drawer of your desk, collecting dust. You want those cards out in circulation!

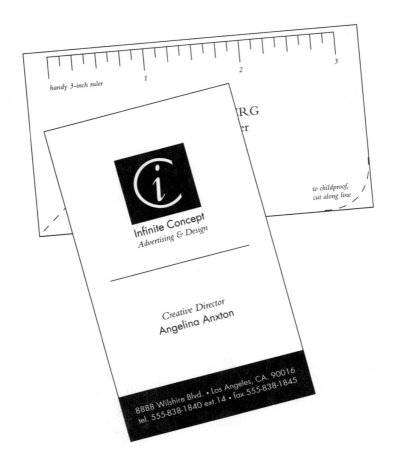

handy 3-inch ruler

1   2   3

RG
er

to childproof,
cut along line

Infinite Concept
Advertising & Design

Creative Director
Angelina Anxton

8888 Wilshire Blvd. • Los Angeles, CA. 90016
tel. 555-838-1840 ext.14 • fax 555-838-1845

PART II

PERSONALIZED PRESENTATIONS

So at this point, you have a card, and you know who you want to give it to, but you don't know how to give it to him or her in the way that will be most effective. Do you just flash your best smile, place it in the recipient's hand, and pray? Or is there another way you can guarantee that the card will be a success? There is, and it's all in the delivery.

33

LET THE GAMES BEGIN

Clever Quotes and Notes

Giving out your business card is like a little game. It could be at a face-to-face meeting, or attached to a note or letter. If the recipient keeps it, shows it to others, refers to it, keeps it in a file, Rolodex™, or somewhere where they can find it easily, well, then you win. If they start folding it in half right away, or throw it away just as soon as you're out of range, then you lose. Sometimes you win. Sometimes you lose. But the more memorable the experience, the better your chances of winning.

One of the easiest ways to make your card stand out is to simply write on the front "See Back." And on the back, write a little note to your recipient containing something of special interest. It could be a Web site they might want to access, a stock tip, a formula, a phone number besides yours they might want to keep, or just a personal note from you. Be creative.

How about a motivational quote pre-printed or handwritten on the back of your business card? Something your client or customer might want to keep on his or her desk, or where it can be easily accessed in a desk drawer. There are hundreds of thousands of quotes to pick from. Check your local library or browse through the reference section of your local bookstore.

It could be your own quote, it could be biblical or sports related, or it could be a quotation from somebody famous in their field. You want to be careful about anything controversial. Too religious, political, or sexual will have an adverse effect. Here are ten ideas to get you started, but remember, the ideas are endless.

1. "Luck is a matter of preparation meeting opportunity." (Oprah Winfrey)

2. "Success usually comes to those who are too busy to be looking for it." (Henry David Thoreau)

3. "There are no secrets to success; don't waste time looking for them. Success is the result of perfection, hard work, learning from failure, loyalty to those for whom you work, and persistence." (General Colin Powell)

4. "If you can dream it, you can do it." (Walt Disney)

5. "The will to win isn't nearly as important as the will to prepare to win." (Bobby Knight)

6. "Imagination is as important as education." (Einstein)

7. "Quality is not an act. It's a habit." (Aristotle)

8. "Kind words can be short and easy to speak, but their echoes are truly endless." (Mother Teresa)

9. "To attain excellence, you must care more than others think is wise, risk more than others think is safe, dream more than others think is practical." (Unknown)

10. "When you reach for the stars, you may not quite get one, but you won't come up with a handful of mud, either."
(Leo Burnett)

I remember getting a business card that had printed on the back "We don't stop playing because we get old, we get old because we stop playing." I kept it on my desk for twenty years. The company is out of business now. I still keep their card.

34

A PERFECT MATCH

Presentation: Paper Clips, Gift Boxes, and Ribbon

A good portion of the time you won't be face-to-face with the person who receives your business card. You'll end up mailing it with a letter, a note, or a package. If you're mailing it with a letter, it could fall out of the envelope as soon as it's opened up. If it's with a package, you want to make sure that it's found and noticed. If you're going to use a paper clip to attach your business card to a letter, try using a gold paper clip. They cost a little more and can be found in some of the better office supply stores or paper product catalogs. Gold paper clips create a better impression than ordinary paper clips, and they stand out. Gold paper clips look classy.

If you're sending a wrapped package or gift to your client or customer, how about a separate box inside for your business card? If what you're sending is valuable, make your business card look valuable as well. You could put your business card inside a small box with two layers of cotton, similar to the ones found in jewelry stores. Tissue paper will work as well. If you've got a sharp, clever, creative card (and you should have one, or go to the back of this book) it will look like a million bucks in a separately wrapped box. Maybe with a clever note explaining how valuable your card can be.

Also, instead of just including your card with a package, think about using a hole-punch to put a hole in the corner of your card where there is no printing. Then take a ribbon and run it through the hole in your card, and wrap the ribbon around the box. Your card won't get lost, they'll have to remove the ribbon to open the box, and your card will get a little more "face time" than it might have had otherwise.

If your business cards match your letterhead, you might want to attach one to every letter you write, in spite of the fact that they might have your card already. If they don't match, attach it to a print piece, flyer, brochure, or something else, rather than to the letter. You want to make the best impression you can. Professionalism always commands better prices for what you do or sell.

35

STAR SEARCH

Stars and Other Stickers

This is so easy, you'll wonder why you haven't seen it before. Buy a box of paste-on stars from your local stationery store. Gold stars are preferred. Then adhere a gold star next to your name on your business card. Your recipient will see you took a little extra time in sending or giving your card. They don't come from the printer this way. The star calls immediate attention to your name.

The stick-ons you can use are endless. It could be a smiley face, a cartoon character, or a sports sticker. It depends on the nature of your business and the nature of the person you're giving your card to. Just use a little imagination. Make your card stand out from everybody else's. Stars can be a nice touch.

The idea is not just to dress up your card with a stick-on. The idea is to make it look individualized, to show that you took the time to do something special on your card exclusively for the person you're sending or giving your card to.

Remember though, this is not *Sesame Street*. Don't go overboard. One star, carefully placed is clever. Many stars could look juvenile. Be creative, but use some subtlety.

36

PERSONALIZATION AT ITS BEST

Signatures, Titles, and Other Personalizing Touches

Save some space on your card to write something personal if the opportunity comes up. And that doesn't just mean on the back. The more personalized your card is, the more apt it is to be saved.

Personalization doesn't mean having a business card with a line on it where your name is supposed to go, and then writing in your name with a stubby pencil when someone asks for your card. Personalization is something out of the ordinary that could make your recipient smile. Save some space to personalize your cards one at a time . . . and that also doesn't mean writing in your name after crossing out the name on somebody else's card.

How about your signature on your business card? Your signature already printed in your own handwriting, in the middle of your card. This is not something you would do if you have a sloppy signature. But if you write nicely, it's something you might want to consider.

Another way to personalize your card is with your title . . . if you have a title. Or maybe put your job position or your company role under your name. If you're not a CEO, president, vice president, or manager, maybe you could personalize your cards with something that at least gets a smile, or a second notice. The computer industry is getting to be the best with interesting titles, as insignificant or semi-serious as they may be. One CEO refers to himself as "Sultan" on his business cards. Another one is "Grand Poobah."

Allen Klein, an author, speaker, and humor educator from San Francisco, refers to himself as a "Jolly-tologist." The title appears under his name, with a simple clown face on the back. Eric Leiser at Gemini Bicycle and Fitness Center in Canton, Ohio, is "VP, Interplanetary Sales." The owners of Gemini say "they don't pay a lot, but they do give great titles." His co-worker, Ryan Pinkus, Ph.D., is "Doctor of Bikeology."

Other titles on various company business cards:

- Judge, Jury, and Executioner

- Computer Guy

- Designated Hitter

- Piddly-Ass Problem Solver

- Head Honcho

- Chief Yahoo

- Design Guru

- Word Wizard

- Top Dog

You'll get more attention if your business card isn't a clone of every other person's in your type of business. And there's always something you can write in at the spur of the moment to make a special impression.

37

COOL AS YOU WANT TO BE

Silly Titles and Silly Cards

You can find crazy business cards in almost every gift shop in every mall in the country. Spencers Gifts, the joke shops, and the gag-catalog companies make a lot of money selling them. But when using your own cards, think about this: Who are you trying to reach? Who are you trying to impress? Don't go overboard. Sometimes trendy or cute is short-lived. Sometimes too clever is too stupid.

It's one thing to put a funny or clever title on your card that your recipient will relate to, think better of you for, or that will give an idea of what you do. In some cases you can mention it when giving out your card to get your recipient to smile. You might have a little fun at your local bar by putting lines on your card like:

- Wars Fought

- Tigers Tamed

- Drunks Sobered

- Juggling Taught

- Virgins Procured

- Whisky Taste-Tester

- Countries Conquered

- Dragons Vanquished

But writing them in or having them pre-printed will probably not increase your business dramatically. In fact, it might just cause the recipient of your card to find a reason not to do business with you. Watch it.

The Iron Horse Tavern in Otter Lake, New York, gives out business cards with their name and address on it on the front and the words "Gone to p, leave my drink alone" on the back. It's amazing how many people keep them, show them to other people, and use them at other bars. It's okay for them. They're a tavern.

Gary Greenberg is a comic and writer in New York City. His card is very cool. It has his name, what he does, the phone number 212-677-3821, and that's all about himself. Since he has a lot of room left over, he has a "handy 3-inch ruler" printed at the top, dotted lines showing (by rounding the corners) how to "childproof" the card, plus dotted lines showing how to fold a corner for a toothpick. It's a simple black-and-white card. It depicts his personality. Everyone comments about it each time it's given out. Gary's a funny/cool guy. (See page 24 for picture)

But, if you feel the need to be cool, consider the business that you're in. Doctors, lawyers, bank presidents, don't need cool. Musicians, magicians, DJs, writers, entertainers, comics, and cartoonists are cool. If you're in a cool industry or business, show it. If you're not, save it.

38

BOUNCE-BACK BUSINESS

Business Card Coupons and Freebies

If you have an office or store where it is important for you to get people to come through your door, you might want to think about having your business card made in a fold-over style, double-sided with a perforation. The tear-off section could contain a discount, a freebie for coming in, a certificate, or a rebate.

I received a business card from a restaurant with a tear-off that read "20 percent off your next bill when dining with four or more." I never threw the card away. I probably ate there at least four times before I remembered to give them the coupon from the card.

When you hand the card to someone who you would like to have come to your place of business, mention the tear-off section and tell them to just bring it in. If the perque, discount, or rebate has perceived value, they'll probably hang on to the card until they're ready to use it. Or they might give it to someone else. If you're in retail, you could put anything from "Good for 10 percent off your next purchase," to "Bring this in for a free (whatever)."

If you don't want to go the tear-off perforated route, you can simply take your existing card, and attach a peel-off sticker to it. Your stickers could vary depending on what you are trying to sell, market, or promote. If you're a restaurant it could be "Free dessert when bringing in this card," "One free entree when one of equal or greater value is purchased," and so on. You have the stickers printed up ahead of time, and decide when you want to use them, if you want to use them, and what you might be using them for.

Barbara, the manager of a convenience store in Parkersburg, West Virginia, passed out 200 business cards to people she did not recognize as regular customers. On the back of her business card she would write "free regular soft drink or coffee" and sign her name. Then she would tell them that when they came into her convenience store, the soft drink or coffee was on her. Of the 200 cards she gave out, fifty-one came back, a 25.5 percent return. Some who came in and redeemed the card bought other things. Also, many of those customers came back for more visits.

The whole idea is to bring them to your office, your store, or your business . . . either one more time, or for the first time if they haven't done business with you before.

39

MONEY TALKS

Using Money with Business Cards

Coins glued with rubber cement to a business card get attention. They get noticed, and they don't get thrown away right away. There is a retailer of a well-known Japanese electronic product who gives out business cards with a Japanese yen glued to the front. On the card is printed "We've got a yen to get you in the store." A restaurant gives the people who made an advance reservation one of their cards with a quarter glued to it. It reads "Thanks for making a reservation. Here's your quarter back for making the phone call." (For areas where pay phones are more than a quarter, the additional coin(s) will make a significant impression.)

One of the most creative cards is paper, and the size of actual U.S. currency. Only instead of a dollar bill, it's a million-dollar bill on the front with the business information on the back. Gene Dowdle in Atlanta, Georgia, is the creator of the million-dollar bill idea and if you call him at 800-462-3443, and ask nicely, I bet he'll send you one for free.

There's a nursery that gives out business cards with a shiny new dime glued to the front. The caption reads, "Money doesn't grow on trees, but betcha 10¢ our trees will appreciate more than this dime will."

Now, these are cards you probably won't give out a hundred at a time. But if you're selective, and you choose your recipients carefully, that small investment could come back a thousand-fold.

It depends on your product, your business, and how much you want attention called to your business card. Coins can be a nice touch.

40

HEY, YOU NEVER KNOW

Lottery Tickets

Bill Evertz, a financial advisor from Upstate New York has his business cards cut the same size as a New York State Lottery ticket. When he hands out his card, he clips it to a lottery ticket. He also puts the following words on the back of his card:

> My professional goal for this year is to assist my clients in wealth accumulation, and financial security through professional competence and personal caring.
>
> I look forward to the possible opportunity of helping you achieve your financial goals during the coming year.
>
> I hope the attached will get you off to the right start!
>
> Bill

Tell them you bought the ticket for both of you. It only costs a buck, and you might not only get your customer's attention, he might even let you share in the winnings.

A lottery ticket has more of an impact than even attaching an actual dollar to your card. With a lottery ticket you get a dollar and a dream. They have to do something with it before they throw it away. It gets people's attention, it shows you have an interest in your recipient, and it's a lot of fun as well. It's even more fun if it's a winner.

41

YOU MAY HAVE ALREADY WON . . .

Your Own Little Contest

This is not the *Reader's Digest* Sweepstakes, Publishers Clearing House, or American Family Publishers ruse. It's a pretty good idea and nobody will complain to the Attorney General. If you run a retail store, or have an office where getting customers to visit is important, here's something you might want to try. You can have sequential numbers put on the back of every one of your business cards. You can start with 1,000 and run it up to however many you feel like printing. You can also buy a progressive number rubber stamp to do the same thing, but it doesn't look as professional.

If you give out a card when you're away from your store or office, tell the recipient that each week you post a number. And you'd like them to come in to check if their number matches the number posted. If it matches, they will have won a (whatever).

The prize can be something small like dinner for four, or movie tickets, or something larger like a computer or DVD player. The idea is simply that they won't throw the card away immediately, and will end up visiting your store or office.

This is a great idea for mall shows, trade shows, boat shows, auto shows, RV shows, sport shows, and any type of consumer event show. It's also great for conventions, industry gatherings, and any type of event where it is important to talk to your card recipient one more time.

You don't have to have a number on every single card you give out. Have two sets. One set for the normal course of everyday business and another set with numbers where you have less of a chance of ever seeing the person again.

It works for Publisher's Clearing House. Only you don't have to give away millions of dollars. Something of any perceived value will do.

YOU HAVE ALREADY WON!

Assorted Freebies to Get Attention

This is one better than "You May Have Already Won." This is "You Have Already Won!" You give out your card, and on the back is something to the effect that "all they have to do is stop by and see you and pick up a _____!"

Ed Riggs, an automobile salesperson from Des Moines, Iowa, has the following words on the back of his business cards:

Congratulations! You have already won dinner for four at McDonalds! It's on us for being a preferred customer. And when you come down to pick up your certificates, enjoy a test drive in the brand new Ford Explorer. No obligation of course. Bring the whole family.

Ed wants the whole family to come in and see him, of course. The Ford Explorer is a family car. The certificates are less than $10 total. Not everyone comes in to pick them up. But his closing ratio is an amazing 35 percent with the people that do show up.

This is great for people who are serious potential customers, and who you have to see one more time. Again, you can have two sets of cards. One with "You Have Already Won," and another set with just a blank reverse side.

43

RICHARD, DICK, RICHIE, OR RICH?

Nicknames on Cards

If you're known by your nickname, you might want it to be on your card. If you name is Hector, but everybody calls you Bud, you'll probably want your clients and customers to do the same. You can list Hector "Bud" Jones, or just Bud Jones, but listing Hector Jones, and telling the person who receives your card to call you Bud, might not be remembered. Depending on your business, you don't want to be too formal. You want to make friends. You want to do business.

Nothing's worse than someone calling your office, asking for you by your regular name and the receptionist only knows you by your nickname. Next thing you know they're saying they don't know who you are.

If your company supplies you with business cards, and your "common everyday nickname" is not printed on the front, do it yourself. Print it nicely over your name. Put quotes around it. Call attention to it.

This makes a nice story. You can say "My friends call me Bud, I hope you'll do the same." "I wrote it on the card." Use your nickname to your best advantage. That's assuming it's a suitable nickname for business. If it's "Stinky," "Waddles," or "Geezer," give it a second thought.

I FORGOT MY CARDS

Examples of Business Card Substitutes

Mike Diehl, a music dealer in New Jersey, often runs out of cards, or decides that maybe giving out a card will not have the right effect. He keeps a large checkbook filled with checks that he doesn't use, just for this purpose. He says that he doesn't have a card at his fingertips but he does have something with the name, address, and phone number of his store. He goes to the checkbook, tears out a check, then tears it in half, leaving the address, and phone number intact. He then writes his name above the store name and says, "Here, keep this. It's the information you need." If the customer has been shopping around, and has two or three business cards already, this really stands out.

Another retailer in the Midwest doesn't use business cards at all. When a customer asks for a card, he takes a plain white 3 x 5 or 4 x 6 index card, then letters it with a black felt tip pen. He patiently prints his name, store name, and phone number on the card while the customer watches every move, then hands it to them saying: "This is the information you requested. I appreciate you coming in, and want to make sure this card doesn't get mixed in with everyone else's when you get home."

There's a car salesperson from Virginia who loves to tell people he doesn't have a business card with him when they ask for his card outside his showroom. He takes a five dollar bill from his wallet, rips it in half, writes his name and phone number on one half, and theirs on the other. He gives the half with his name on it to the person looking for his card. Then he simply says "When you come in to see me, I'll give you the other half." It's worth five dollars to him to get another prospect into the showroom, and he's got their name on the other half of the bill in case he needs to call them to come in.

Don't make a "My new cards aren't ready . . . hand me your cocktail napkin" first impression. Business cards don't have to look like business cards. It's all part of being a bit more creative when giving out your name and address. Don't always write on the first thing you can grasp that can be written on.

45

14-KARAT CUSTOMERS

Two Set Trick—One Set New, One Set Old

I did a program recently for Kawasaki dealers on small budget advertising and zero-cost PR. That's where I met Duke Schmidt, a motorcycle dealer in Fairfield, Iowa. He has a great way of handing out business cards. He has two different kinds. An ordinary card with black type, and a gold, elaborate business card with a stylish font, and a very shiny finish. You can practically see your face in it, it's so shiny. The black and white card is, well, at best . . . ordinary, not to mention a little smudgy.

As Duke explained it to me, when he is selling a motorcycle and the prospect asks for a card, he pulls the cards out of his pocket. There are several of the black and white cards on top. Dirty, ragged, oil-stained business cards. On the bottom is the gold card. Shiny, new, and very clean. His prospect obviously sees the dirty black and white cards first. But then Duke says: "You're very important to me. I want you to come back to buy a bike. You're a gold card customer. I want to make sure you have one of the gold cards. Don't lose it. They're special. When do you think you might be back in?"

Okay. Maybe not everybody can get away with it. But giving out a business card creatively can make all the difference between new business, more business, or no business. You want to make it memorable.

46

IS THAT THE PHONE?

Ringing Telephone Card Holders

Business card holders make your business card look special. It makes them more memorable, makes them look important. One of the more clever ones out there right now has been developed by Clegg Industries in Torrance, California. This is a small 3 x 4 $\frac{1}{2}$ inch, all-black, high-gloss folder. The outside of the folder is printed with "When You're Looking for the Very Best . . ." When you open it up, the inside reads "Give me a ring" with your business card displayed. And guess what? A telephone rings! Not a real phone, just the sound of a phone ringing. They put a little computer chip in the card.

Business card holders that ring. We use them ourselves. Clients love them. It's a great attention-getter (and could probably increase your social life about 20 percent as well). And it's a great way to keep your card from getting lost in somebody's drawer. It's a clever concept that never fails to bring a smile and a "Well, would you look at that!" to the lips of the recipient.

The best part is that these beauties never get filed away to be lost forever in business card "Never-Never Land." On the contrary, people who receive them tend to carry them around and show all their friends this novel little item. You could end up getting dozens of calls from people who just want to know where you got it. And if you play your cards right, you can turn those callers into prospects—or at least get some fresh referrals out of them.

Obviously, you're not going to give one of these to every single person you meet. You may want to save them for really hot prospects or for situations where you need that extra "something" that will keep your name out above your competitors. But a little ingenuity can give you more mileage on these items than you can imagine.

Consider using them as (or with) a direct mail piece for a targeted group of very hot prospects. In a separate letter, or handwritten directly on your card, include a message that the prospect will receive a free gift or a special discount for bringing the card (with holder) back to your store, showroom, or office. Not only do you get a chance to sell to that prospect face-to-face, you've got the card holder back to use again and again.

There's practically no limit to the way these holders can be used, and certainly no limit to the type of business they would be appropriate for.

One great match was with a telecommunications rep who left one of these with every promising prospect she met in person. She was tickled by the phone reference and is lobbying to require her whole sales team to carry them.

But it doesn't have to be that kind of literal connection. The telephone is a universal means of conducting business. These holders have been used by everyone from surgeons to snowmobile dealers. One enterprising mom even ordered them for her college-age daughters so they could make themselves memorable to eligible young men!

By the way: If you want a sample of the ringing telephone card holder call 1-800-724-9700 ext. 110. They'll send you one free. Tell them you saw it in this book.

47

HIGHLIGHTING FOR A REAL IMPRESSION

Highlighting, Circling, and Calling Attention to Specifics

Always carry a highlighter and a black felt tip pen with you in a business situation. Calling attention to a specific part of your business card can make the difference between whether someone keeps your card and uses the information, or whether it ends up in the trash.

If you want someone to call you back at a specific phone number, highlight it. Call their attention to it. If your mission statement is on your card, and it's important that they know it, highlight it.

Maybe your area code has changed. Circle it with a black felt tip pen. Maybe you want to circle your name so they call you at your company and nobody else. Maybe there are two addresses on your card and you want to check or highlight the one they need to send information to.

The idea here is to be a little bit more dramatic than pulling out a stubby pencil to write on your card with. A highlighter shows that you're on a different level business wise. Not everyone carries one in his or her pocket or purse. And a black felt tip pen makes a better impression when using it to write on a business card. The cost of the pens is negligible. The effect can be huge.

48

KEEP ON CLIPPING

Clipping Articles to Put with Your Cards

One great idea for getting your client's, customer's, or prospect's attention, is to send them or bring them something that is of interest to them from a newspaper or magazine. When my daughter's engagement appeared in the local paper, one of our vendors clipped it out and sent it to me (not her) with their card and a note saying "You must be happy and proud!" I liked it. It showed they went out of their way. Clipping articles from publications is a great way of establishing rapport.

Here's where your business card plays an important part. Attach your business card to the article with the back-side out. This is where you write your personal note.

This is definitely one time you don't want to staple your card to the article. Use a paper clip so they can easily remove your card. All your pertinent information is on the front, and they'll turn it over, even if it's just out of curiosity.

So don't keep all those great ideas you find in trade publications, local and national newspapers, or newsstand magazines to yourself. Cut them out. Think about who they might be of interest to. Send them with your business card. You'll be amazed at the response you'll get.

49

GOTCHA!

Catching Someone's Attention

You've heard it before. And you're going to hear it again: "You never get a second chance to make a great first impression." You get one shot. Don't blow it when handing out a business card. One of the problems when giving out a card is that sometimes we don't make it any big deal. The conversation is over, you say, "Here's my card," and then it's pretty much over. You start to walk away into oblivion. Or you present your business card at the start of the conversation. That can sometimes be a wrong move because then your recipient has to take the time to look it over, or not look at it at all. You lose the continuity, the spontaneity, and the pizzazz. Make your card a big deal. Make it a big deal, even if it's not.

There's a magician who works corporate events with a very special business card. He gives you a card, and when you reach for it, it goes up in smoke. He then gives you a second one that doesn't. Now that's memorable.

Stress cards as business cards are great. (Most premium incentive companies have them in their catalogs.) The person puts their thumb on them and you can show them that the color that appears will tell how stressed they are. Great conversation piece. (It could also tell you if they're comfortable with you at the moment.) Don't give your card in an effort to get away from someone. It has a negative effect. Make sure your recipient feels that your card has value, that it's worth something.

If you want to get someone's attention while giving them your card, hand it to them, then keep it between your thumb and forefinger. Don't let go. You can always say "Sure you want this?" or "You're not going to throw it away are you?" At least you get attention called to your card. A little personality, cleverness, and humor can go a long way.

50

THE W. C. FIELDS APPROACH
TO BUSINESS CARDS

Being Persistent

There's a great quote accredited to W. C. Fields: "If at first you don't succeed, try, try again. And then if you don't succeed . . . quit. There's no sense in being a damn fool about it."

This is where high drama has its place. It's especially effective in an office situation. You're sitting on one side of a desk, your client or customer is sitting on the other side.

They ask for a card. You give them a card. Then the conversation starts to go the other way. What you thought was positive turns negative. You thought you had a shot at their business, and the next thing you know, they're taking a shot at you. How do you react?

When you give out your business card, leave it on their desk. It will probably stay there while you're in your client's or customer's office. Generally they don't immediately put it in their pocket, or file it. It stays there, right in plain sight. Sometimes they look at it first, then put it down.

If you start to hear statements like: "Your price is way too high, we're not in a position to work with you, besides we have no money." or "I don't know, we're over budget for this year, and next year's budget looks worse. Could we return what we bought last month?" or "We've done business with your company before and have had bad results. At our last meeting we were told not to do any more business with you."

Then you might want to consider thanking them for their time, picking up your card and putting it in your pocket. Fold it in half. Quietly tear it in half if you want to. Head for the door. If you simply take your card back (mind you this is without asking if you can have it back), one of two things is going to happen:

1. The person on the other side of the desk will be shocked and start to make positive comments. Then you can simply take out a new card (or the same one from your pocket), and put it back down on the desk. Or put it in his or her hand.

2. The person on the other side of the desk will actually become more negative and you probably shouldn't be doing business with them anyway.

Think about your performance as if you were trying for an academy award. Do it with some flair.

51

STUPIDITY SELDOM WORKS

A Time and Place for Comedy

Imagine that you're buying a new car. You're looking at a car that stickers at $35,000 or more. You tell the salesperson you want to think about it. You might be back. You ask for their card.

All of a sudden this mature, responsible salesperson decides he might do better as a stand-up comic. He pulls a number of business cards out of his pocket. He shuffles them. He fans them out and says "Here, pick a card, any card." You pick a card and he says "Oops, sorry, wrong card. You have to pick again." Then he palms a card and pulls it out of your ear. Giving out a card is not schtick unless you're a person that does schtick. If you're an entertainer that's one thing. If you're not, it could be stupid.

Handing out or exchanging business cards is not to be taken lightly if actually creating business is important to you. At a party or social situation comic routines are one thing. In a business setting stupidity doesn't lend itself to making a good impression.

Think of the person who you're giving your card to as your mother or grandmother. How do you do it so she understands your business, who you are, and the fact that you care about her?

Make it a memorable experience, so when they look at your card again when they're out of your sight, they recall a memorable experience.

52

I'LL SEND IT TO YOU

Getting Someone's Home Address Can Be Revealing

You have to decide for yourself exactly how important it is to gain more information about the person who asks you for a card. It depends on the type of business you're in, and it also depends on how early in the conversation the need for a card comes up. If someone asks for your card too soon, it might be a ploy for them to get out of the conversation quickly. If you feel that by giving someone a card, they'll quickly disappear, you might want to consider not giving them one. In fact, just by telling them you'll send them one in tonight's mail, it will at least ensure you an address.

An address tells a lot of things about a person. The area where they live tells you something about their station in life, it indicates whether they live in a house or an apartment, and if you have other clients or customers in that area, it gives you of a possible common denominator . . . you might know the same people.

Many people who ask you for a card don't have a card of their own. So by telling them you'll send them one in the mail, you not only get an address, it's an easy way of getting their name as well. And a good percentage of the time that name will also be listed in the phone book, so now you have a phone number as well. And that all starts by saying "I don't have a business card with me, but I'd sure like to send you one. Let me have your address and I'll make sure you get it."

The problem when someone asks us for a business card, is that many times we are just too eager to give it to them. Relax. Take a moment. Count to ten. Think about how giving them a card is going to help you with more business. How much more do you need to know about the person before they get your card? And if you need to know quite a bit more and feel that information might not be readily forthcoming, that's a perfect time for, "I'll send one out in tonight's mail. May I have your address?"

53

MY CARD, MY JOB, MY RESUME

Resume Cards

If your current job is a stepping-stone, a transition job, or if you are between jobs, here's something you may never have thought of. It's a resume that looks like a business card, and it's a business card as well.

When applying for a new job, particularly in person, it's nice to get to know the person who's interviewing you before handing them your resume. If it's someone who you haven't met before, you hand them a resume and for the next five minutes they're reading your resume and not talking to you. If the major points are on a card first, they can scan the card, talk to you a bit, and then read your resume.

The other nice thing about having a business card resume is that you never know who you might be talking to who could be interested in you for a job. It could be at a party, in line at the theater, or in a parking lot. Somebody might say, "It's nice to see you," and ask, "What are you doing now?" You hand them a card, mention that you are considering various opportunities, and you go your separate ways. The card stays with them containing information as to:

• current address and phone number

• skills and qualifications

- references

- anything else pertinent to what you're looking for, or might be suited for

You can have a one-side card, two-side with references on the back, or a folded card with previous job history and outstanding skills, traits, and qualifications. You could even consider a three-fold card that unfolds to a small brochure. You might even include approximate salary you're looking for. You can be as bold or creative as you want to be. It's your card.

54

RUBBER STAMPS AND BUSINESS CARDS

The Flexibility of Rubber Can't Be Beat

If the back of your business card is blank, you might want to consider a variety of rubber stamps that you can imprint on the blank side. Rubber stamps can use different color ink pads, and they can be better than having ten different cards printed for ten different types of clients or customers.

Dan Bortolan of the Chimney Sweep Co. located in Hamden, Connecticut, uses a rubber stamp that is a cartoon character of a hand tipping a top hat with the words "It's really nice to meet you!" underneath. The nice part is that it fits his personality.

Dan Jacobsen, a bicycle dealer from Vermont has a new stamp made up every time he takes on a new line, or is offering a new special. It's like updating his business card by the day, the week, and the month. Here are ten different rubber stamp ideas for the back of your business card.

1. Good for one free_____.
   Offer expires_____.

2. Save 10 percent on your next purchase with this card.
   Offer expires_____.

3. Check out our new Web site at

www._____

4. My personal line is _____.
Feel free to call me direct.

5. Our 800 number is _____.

6. If you'd like more information, write your name and
address here and send this card back to me.

_____

_____

7. In case of any emergency, my cell phone
number is_____.

8. I will be on vacation from _____ to _____.
Call and ask for _____ while I'm gone.

9. Here's a new service you might not be aware of:

_____

_____

10. We now also stock:

_____

_____

The idea with using a rubber stamp or a number of rubber
stamps on the back of your business card is that you can keep changing the information without continually reprinting your cards. You
can personalize it, for the day, the week, or the month. It also shows
a bit more professionalism than writing everything in longhand.

55

CARDS THAT AREN'T CARDS

Giving Gifts or Premiums Instead of Cards

Your name, address, company name, phone number, and so on, can go on any type of premium item, but they're not always a substitute for a creative business card.

The point of giving away premiums imprinted with your information is, of course, so that they will be kept. Popcorn packets with your information on the wrapper are cute, but once the popcorn is popped, how many people are going to keep the wrapper?

Desk accessories can be a good choice. Imprinted pens are historically popular, but provide little room for imprinting and are likely to get lost in a drawer with others of their kind. Consider instead a penholder, which would leave more room for your name and logo and would be within view more constantly than the pens it holds.

Also keep in mind that your premium will have more impact and be remembered longer if it actually relates to the nature of your business. An imprinted bookmark, for instance, would be a questionable choice for a direct satellite provider.

- A southern California independent financial advisor gives out small pocket calculators "to keep track of your accumulated wealth" with his name, telephone number, and e-mail address.

• One travel agent prefers to keep prospects thinking about her and her services by handing out specially printed luggage tags.

• A popular building contractor leaves his promising prospects with a tape measure that is imprinted with his company information on both sides and helpful tips on home design printed across the first eight feet of the tape.

Many businesses have made themselves memorable by choosing a premium in the "cute" category. Stress balls in a vast array of shapes and office "toys" like puzzles or brain-teasers are options that are both functional and fun.

Some other options to consider are:

• golf bag tags

• pocket calendars

• checkbook covers

• business card cases

• CD ROM holders

• first aid kits

• coffee mugs

• clocks

There are hundreds of places that sell premium items. The list is endless; the ideas are endless as well. You can start by doing a search on the Internet.

No matter what the value or perceived value of the premium you give, never let it stand alone. Always give or attach a "regular" business card along with it. The premium's primary function is to make the prospect think about you in a positive way and to reinforce your name and message in his or her mind. But your regular card should always be left so that it can be kept on file as it usually would.

HalJoe custom coach builders gives out a very unique business card. It looks like a bus. Actually it is a bus. A model of a tour bus that has their company identification on the sides and on the back. It actually rolls. The sides just read HalJoe custom coach, pretty much like a touring rock group would have it. That's their market. On the back are the phone and fax numbers, plus an e-mail address. They feel an address is unimportant. People will call if interested. Joe of HalJoe carries these busses . . . er cards, in a special bag that fits onto his briefcase. Once you get a bus, you can't stick it in your pocket, you don't want to set it down, and you definitely don't want to throw it out. So you carry it around. People ask, "Whatcha got there?" It's very cool.

56

KEEP IT CLEAN

Business Card Cases

The problem with keeping business cards in our pockets is that they can get bent, wrinkled, or soiled. Men put them in the back pants pocket, then sit on them in the car. They appear bent and warped when the time comes to give them out. Women put them in their purses, along with a variety of things that may stain or smudge them.

Spend a couple of dollars and get yourself a business card case. You can find these at just about any office supply store, or any place that engraves gifts. You can have your name put on the case for very little cost. There are a variety of sizes, styles, and colors. There are business card cases that look like little brief cases. There are card cases that have money clips attached. There are black ones, gold ones, silver ones, and plastic ones. They have a great, simple purpose. They keep your cards looking new.

When someone asks you for a card, when you take the business card case out of your pocket, you really show some class by letting your recipient see how much you care about the condition of your card. It's much better than taking a stack of cards with a rubber band around them out of your pocket. And it certainly is better than giving out a card that is dog-eared, stained, or bent.

57

WHEN YOU'RE SMILING

Presentation Cleverness

Lighten up. Don't act like digging out a business card is a chore. Smile, and the world smiles with you. People remember people who make them happy.

Charlie Donavan, a kitchen and bath dealer in the Midwest, always has a smile on his face. He likes to make people laugh, and when a customer says "Do you have a card?" he says, "Yes, they're a quarter. Or three for fifty cents. How many do you want?"

Ray Wilson, a store owner in Oregon, sometimes says to his customers who ask for a card, "I lose more sales by giving out cards. This isn't going to cost me a sale is it? Is there some way you can make a decision now?"

Dorothy Michalson in Tampa, Florida, has her cards on bright yellow stock with a happy-face printed on the back. She's in the flower business and her slogan is "Flowers make for a happy day." Happiness shows on her cards.

Mary Lee Snyder sells a line of custom furniture in New York. She keeps a roll of un-circulated pennies in her desk drawer (you can buy them for face value). She tapes a bright and shiny penny to the back of her card, hands it to a customer who doesn't place an order on the spot, and says "this is a penny for your thoughts. I would really appreciate you thinking about ordering this as soon as possible. You're going to love it!"

Bob and David Donovich in Colorado own a microbrewery, and they actually have ten sets of business cards between them. Each set has a different joke on the back, with the header that says "Stop me if you've heard this. . . ." People save them, they pass them around. Each joke is only three lines each. They aren't readily tossed out. People show them, they talk about them, and they remember them. And when someone says "Hey, where'd you hear that?" The person can say, "It was on the back of this card! "

Whatever works for you. Any way you can get your client or customer to smile is a plus.

58

IT'S NOT BRAIN SURGERY,
IT'S NOT ROCKET SCIENCE . . .
IT'S COMMON SENSE

A Little Recap

Using your business cards effectively to increase business, find more customers, create more revenue, and keep your name out in the marketplace doesn't have to be hard. It's simple. You have to have a great card. You just have to be a little creative, and a little clever, you need to use some personality, and you have to want to get those cards out there. Remember the basics.

1. You have to have an interesting, creative, clever, appealing, professional business card. If you don't, you don't stand out from the pack.

2. Be sure that the information your client or customer needs to know is on your card. It could be your cell phone number, e-mail address, fax number, a map to your location, toll-free number, or whatever will interest your recipient.

3. Get your recipient's business card, or find out their name and phone number. Ask for their card. If they don't have one, write some notes on the back of your card, cross out the front so you don't give it someone else, and enter the info into your memory or database.

4. Give two cards when someone asks for one. One for themselves, and ask them to give the other to someone else who may be interested in your product or service.

5. Be nice. Use some personality. Have a ten-second commercial ready to use when someone asks for your card.

6. Be interesting. Life is boring only if you are.

7. If you're happy, tell your face. Smile. People are more apt to do business with a happy person.

8. Never give out a soiled card.

9. Find out the name of the person who asks for your card and use it in the conversation. People love to hear their own name.

10. Always be on the lookout for a business card that is better designed, more creative, or better looking than yours. Upgrade often. Never settle for second best.

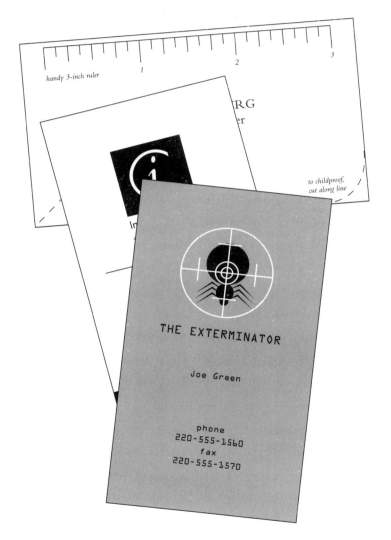

handy 3-inch ruler   1   2   3

RG
er

to childproof,
cut along line

THE EXTERMINATOR

Joe Green

phone
220-555-1560
fax
220-555-1570

PART III

CREATIVE DESIGN . . .
IT'S ALL IN THE CARDS

Here are some ideas for creating a better card, particularly if the one you're using now is . . . well . . . second rate, not well designed, not very creative, or just plain stinks.

59

HOW MUCH IS TOO MUCH?

What Information a Card Needs

In the beginning, business cards began as society calling cards, way before Alexander Bell invented the telephone. It was easy back then. A name on a card, with maybe the city or town with an address where the person resided. If there was no address, they could just go into town and "inquire." Not so anymore. How much information do you really need on your business card? Think about it carefully. Name? Address? Phone number? Home number? Cellular phone number? E-mail address? Web site? Logo? Mission statement? Is your business card starting to turn into a small book? First of all, make yourself a little checklist of the information you might want on your card:

- company name

- company logo

- description of what your company does

- company slogan

- multiple locations

- association or union affiliations

- your name

- any degrees you might have

- position

- street address

- P.O. Box address

- zip code

- business phone number

- your extension number

- separate voice-mail number

- 800 number

- after-hours number

- fax number

- pager number

- home phone number

- cellular phone number

- e-mail address

- Web site address

- dual languages

- location map

Now, go back and start eliminating what you don't need. Then go back and do it once more. Ask yourself a few questions. Will your office number be able to supply the other numbers when called, if you're not there? Will your Web site have more of the information that can't go on the card? What you have left will determine if you need a single or bi-fold business card. Remember, you want to leave room for someone to write down information or notes on your card. Make sure there's space.

Don't load your card with so much information that it looks cluttered. Make your business card a good representation of you and your business, with all the necessary information your recipient will need, but not so much that it is overdone. Don't get carried away with so much that your card is crammed.

Keep in mind that you want to have whatever is on your card follow the natural flow of the eye. Select whatever works well together. Stay away from too many type styles and capital letters. Make sure there's enough white space, and if it starts to look too confusing, it probably is.

60

BOTH SIDES NOW

Two Sides or One?

More and more people are starting to use the front and back of their business cards. But which is the front? Which is the back? Is it easy to tell the difference? Where can your customer write notes? This can be a problem, particularly when sending the card in the mail. In person you can hand it front side up. But if both sides are loaded with text, it can be hard to distinguish front from back.

Are you using the back of your card? If so, how? Some companies use it to list their Web sites. Some put a calendar, map, or something pertinent to their business. There's one retailer that simply puts "This Space For Rent." Whatever works for you, I guess.

If you're going to use front and back, make sure your company name and logo (or your name) stands out on the front side. Make it bigger than anything else on the card. That way your recipient will know it's the front. Then if you use the back for a Web site address, slogan, map, or secondary information, keep it small. Leave a lot of white space . . . space to write notes, or just space to identify it as the back of the card.

Keep this in mind: Most people won't know there is something on the back unless you bring it to their attention. When giving out the card you might have to actually tell the recipient about the information that's on the back. Turn it over. Show them. If you send it in the mail, they may never look on the back. You might even have to write "see back" on the front of the card. Something else, when people store business cards, when they put them in their pocket or desk drawer, they forget which ones have information on the back. They might see it once, then forget to look again.

So use a little discretion. The back side of your card can be useful and valuable. It can work for you as long as your recipient knows it's there, that there are two printed sides, and they know which is the front and which is the back.

61

CREATIVE IDEAS FOR
THE BACK OF YOUR CARD

Relevant Information to Increase Your Card's Value

So if you're convinced that the back of your business card could be a great place for putting information that could be relevant to your client or customer's interest or industry, there are a number of things that could go on the back. How about something on your card to compute interest, win at Blackjack, or figure wattage or horsepower? The ideas are endless and the value could be priceless.

One of the better ideas I found comes from Jerry Teplitz Enterprises in Virginia Beach, Virginia. Jerry is a speaker on "Managing the Stress of Change." His business card is pretty standard on the front, with the exception of the outline of a human head with a star emanating from the brain section. On the back are two outlines of a person's skull, one side view and the other rearview. The words read "SHIATSU Headaches and Hangovers," and all the pressure points are highlighted on the person's head. Jerry reports that he's come across his business card carried by people who still have it five years after his program.

C&C Offset Printing Co., Ltd., a Chinese and American print shop, has a business card that lists weights for common papers in Hong Kong. Unique idea. There's no end to the number of things you can put on the back of a business card that your recipient would consider valuable.

For example:

- a calendar for the current year

- home mortgage loan interest tables

- Las Vegas odds on various games

- metric conversion tables

- a chart for calculating 15 percent and 20 percent tips

- phone numbers for all the major airlines

- a calorie table

- a local sports team's schedule

- postal information

- recipes

- international monetary conversion tables

Dr. John B. Carbery, DMD in Yakima, Washington, gives out a Flosscard™ with his name and office address. If you haven't seen them, these cards are just slightly thicker than regular cards, but have dental floss that pulls out through a little hole. Perfect for Dentists and Orthodontists.

There's a printing company in Jupiter, Florida, that explains how the printing press was developed. (It was invented by Johannes Gutenberg who got the idea from watching a wine press in action.)

This is explained on the back of their card in detail. Perfect idea for a printer.

Whatever idea you have for the back of your card that someone would value has to be relevant to your business. And it should open the door to more conversation about using your product or service. Something you can talk about as you hand a person your card.

The past few years have seen tremendous growth in the popularity of health and healing. People clamor for information about traditional cures, homeopathic remedies, alternative medicine, mind-body healing, herbalism, Ayurvedic healing traditions, acupuncture, hypnotherapy, positive visualizations, and the medicinal power of laughter. You name it—it's out there and people want it.

Business cards that can help you feel better are a hot commodity. People seem to carry them around or save them forever. The possibilities are endless. Business cards with homeopathic remedies for headaches, backaches, colds, or cards that measure stress have real staying power.

A New York City company called MJ Graphics, Inc., 800-988-2685, carries quite an array of health-related cards. They can provide you with everything from first aid checklists to headache prevention cards to stress indicators to Diet Buster™ habit control cards.

But don't limit yourself to what's already available. Anything you can dream up can be easily fit to your card. Why not a diagram of pressure points (licensed massage therapist) or a guide to proper stretching techniques (sporting goods manufacturer)?

Of course it's best to give premiums and novelty cards that actually relate to your business. But try not to think too literally; be creative. A Smoke Buster™ card would be entirely appropriate when given by a life insurance representative. A headache prevention card is clever and memorable coming from a tax preparer.

You can come up with a lot of healthful ideas for the back of your business card from your local public library, on the Internet, or just by taking an informal survey of your family, friends, and associates—ask them what interests them. Or start a contest among your staff or sales reps to see who can come up with the best idea. A little creativity can go a long way in finding an idea that suits your business to a tee. Use it in good health!

62

SOMETIMES LESS IS MORE

Simplicity in Layout Can Be Good

Today there's a lot of information being put on business cards. But people scan cards first, rather than reading them thoroughly. Be concise. Let your customer or client get a complete overview of your card in two seconds or less. Catch their eye. Don't use multiple type styles. Keep the most important information in bold print.

Be artistic as well as creative. And condense as much as possible. Use state abbreviations (NY instead of New York), street abbreviations (Ave. instead of Avenue), and Corporate abbreviations (Inc., Ltd., Co., etc.). Think about using periods instead of dashes in phone numbers (315.422.4488). You can use P for phone, F for fax, H for home, W for work, Cell for cellular. Pgr for pager, and so on.

The easiest way to lay out your card is to first take a 3 x 5 or 5 x 7 index card and start putting all the information on the front side. Use as many abbreviations as you can. Then delete what is non-essential. Then delete some more. How much can you take away, and still have an effective card? Next show the card to someone else and get their opinion. What do they think is unnecessary? Don't just leave the creative ideas to your graphics person or printer. Show it to a relative, a neighbor, or a co-worker. You never know where that next creative business card idea will come from.

63

A PERFECT ANGLE

Using Different Shapes

Al things are not created equal. Business cards don't have to be perfect rectangles. They can be square. They can be oval. They can have an interesting die-cut pattern. They can be clever, have creative slants, use cuts, and contain perforations and holes.

There are unlimited variations of size and shape. But remember people can't easily put an odd-shaped card into their card cases or wallets. Different shaped cards don't stack well with other cards. Unusual shapes can start with just being larger or smaller, by trimming a corner or cutting an edge. You could also consider rounded corners.

The Steep Incline Bike Shop has a business card where the top is cut on a 35° angle. There's a dentist in Phoenix whose business card has a bite mark . . . a bite out of the corner of the card with the outline of teeth marks. There's a Grocer's Association in Oklahoma City whose card looks like a little grocery bag, complete with the corrugated edge on top with half-circle cut out at the top of the bag. Use your imagination.

One of the absolute best business cards that doesn't look like a business card comes from the Senior Vice President of the Fort Wayne National Bank. His business cards look like little checks and he tears them off one at a time from a little pad. Your cards could look like a telephone (if that's your business), or they can look like your product.

These cards are more expensive than standard business cards. But how much are you willing to spend to make an impression?

64

ROLODEX™ PERPLEXED?

Rolodex-Ready Cards

Y ou've seen them before. You probably have a bunch in your desk drawer. These are the cards cut to be stored in a Rolodex file. There are a couple of problems here. Rolodex files come in different sizes. And more and more Rolodexes are being phased out in favor of computer databases. You can scan cards into your computer. Also, some business cards are kept in business card files with little plastic sleeves that are precut. There is no standard size to the number of them on the market. And business cards pre-cut with those nifty little slots to be put into a Rolodex are just plain hard to store with everybody else's card if you keep a stack in your pocket or on your desk. The bottom starts to bend easy because of the holes or slots, and the card starts to look ratty very quickly.

If you're sending a card to someone who you know keeps a Rolodex file, you might want to send it in one of the little plastic sleeves that are already slotted for Rolodex use. Otherwise, don't think that just by having it cut for a Rolodex, your card is going to stay around longer. Chances are it will just be thrown away a little quicker.

If you still have clients who use Rolodex revolving files, you should consider two sets of cards. One set with the cut outs, just for these people, and a set for everyone else. Do your own little survey of the people you might be sending or giving your cards to. Find out how they store business cards. This will quickly tell you what route might be the most advantageous to you.

There is a simple way to go about this, when you already have two sets of cards, one set Rolodex cut, and the other standard. Simply ask, "Do you use a Rolodex?" If they don't, forget the fancy cuts.

65

TEN THINGS YOU NEVER WANT TO SEE ON A BUSINESS CARD

They Aren't As Obvious As You Think

Check out the business cards in your pocket. How do they look? Bright and clean? A little worn and wrinkled? Business cards are a reflection of yourself and your business. You are what you hand out. Here are some things you *don't* want to see on them.

1. Creases and bent edges. A business card with "dog ears" or any type of fold from being in your pocket too long should never be given out. It looks bad. You might want to consider getting a business card case to fit in your pocket or purse, just to protect the cards and make them appear special. You're special aren't you? Your business cards should be too.

2. Typos. It's common sense. Typos look stupid. But you'd be surprised at how many times business cards aren't examined after they come back from the printer. Does your phone number have all the correct digits? Are your area and zip codes correct? Take a good look before you start passing them out. Joe Driesel, owner of Driesel Lumber Co. in Albion, New York, received free business cards from one of his suppliers. The first batch came without a phone number. He said "this fact was, unfortunately, pointed out to me by

an irate customer who had to call information to get my number." He had been passing them out for six months and no one had noticed the omission including himself. In other words, check it out right away.

3. Signs of age. Discoloration, fading, yellowing . . . c'mon, just get them redone. Nothing lasts forever. Take a look. If they're too old, throw them out.

4. Written-in names. Never, never, never, hand out a business card with your name written in . . . at least if you're really serious about doing business.

5. Anything crossed out. Don't cross out somebody else's name, correct a typo, change a phone number, or change an area or zip code by crossing out and writing in. Your business card is a reflection of your business. Tacky is as tacky does.

6. Smudges or stains. If it's dirty, don't use it. Remember your mother always said, "Wear clean underwear in case you end up in the hospital?" Never carry soiled business cards with you. Clean cards mean serious business. You never know if it's going to be passed around to someone else.

7. Any type of writing. Don't give out a card that you've ever used to write notes to yourself, or has any kind of previous writing on it. It makes the card look worn, used, dated, and unprofessional.

8. Bleed-through. If you're using the back to promote your Web site, as a calendar, or something relative to your business,

make sure the type doesn't come through to the other side. Caution your printer about this. Any amount of shadow will make your card look dirty.

9. Anything off-color. It's cute around your friends, but how do you know where your card is going to end up? Be careful. Your name is in front of the world . . . or could be. You never know.

10. Staple holes, paper-clip marks. You don't want your business cards to look re-used. You're not on an austerity budget. And if you are, don't let it be known. If it looks recycled, it makes you and your business look recycled as well.

66

SKIP THIS IF YOU'RE NOT PHOTOGENIC

Photo Cards

Pictures on business cards are very big right now, the cost is way down, and they get noticed. They're particularly effective for real estate salespeople, speakers, authors, entertainers, and any type of sales and service business people. Actually, I guess they can be used for just about anybody. You can probably increase your social life (and probably be more memorable at your local bar) if you have a business card with your picture on it, even if you don't use the card for business. But this is a business book. You'll make more of an impression if your picture is in color, rather than black and white. But a two-color card with other than black ink can work too.

Kathie Hightower from Hightower Resources in Tacoma, Washington, has her picture on the front and back of her card in two different poses. The front is Kathie in her business pose, and the back is Kathie starting to take off her Star Trek glasses, with the phrase "It's Time for a New Vision!" It's done on off-white card stock with dark green ink. It's cost effective.

Robyn Henderson, networking specialist from Australia has an outstanding photo card, not only of herself, but one of her book. Robyn warns, however, that photos might distract customers from the most important information, and advises that you "make sure your phone number is in big type so people don't need glasses to see it."

There are a lot of companies that specialize in photo cards. Prince Party Productions in Billings, Montana, puts a picture of their DJ van on their business card, along with their staff. It's really cool. The van is shown with party lights in the background,

> ## Two Companies That Specialize in Photo Cards
>
> Postcards
> 50 West 23rd St., 6th Floor
> New York, NY 10010
> phone: 800-POSTCARDS
>
> Future Imaging Systems
> 5327 Jacuzzi St., Suite 3B
> Richmond, CA 94804
> phone: 800-974-8881

the door open, and five people with smiles surrounding it. The signage on the van shows the business of the company, and it's a nice casual photo showing the personalities of the DJ's. Pictures work. Color makes them better.

If you're going to have your picture on your business card, have it professionally done by a fashion photographer, not a portrait photographer. This is not a picture for your local museum of modern art. This is a picture to reflect you better than you really are. After you have the photographs taken, have your friends pick out the best picture. Your friends are better critics. Then have a professional photo card shop give you some ideas for how to look great on a business card. It could be with shadows, outlines, boxes or any number of different ideas. Or it could be just you in a full body pose, head shot, or from the waist up. If you want to make an impression with your cards don't just take a Polaroid of yourself to your local quick-print. Put some thought into it. Get some experienced help. Spend a few bucks. The dividends will be worth it.

You can also design your business cards to look like baseball trading cards. Depending on your business, it could work. William Cleary, Sr., Account Sales Manager for the Promotion Group in Lansing, Michigan, has his stats on his baseball trading card/business card like someone who is playing major league ball. The nice part about a card like this is that you can put information about yourself including when you started in the business, how long your company has been around, your major clients, any awards you might have won, and extended mission statement. This is great for self-promotion.

Remember though, you've got to decide how you want to be perceived. Serious and corporate? Baseball trading card style-business cards don't make it. High-tech? Go another route. Humorous, contemporary? Casual? Then the trading card thing might work.

If you're a manufacturer who has many reps, you could have a different card for everybody. If you sell sporting goods, this is perfect. If you're a small company with a few salespeople who are close to their customers, the trading card format might work if you have a set of regular business cards as well.

If you're going to do this, take a good look at actual baseball trading cards. Try to simulate the best points. You don't have to be dressed in a baseball jersey with a bat. Be yourself. You can talk about being "part of the team" or being "in the big leagues." You can use these cards for a special promotion, a new product announcement, or for regular business. It's a fun card. It may work for you.

67

BEAM ME UP, SCOTTIE

Holograms

I like holograms, and I like showing them to other people. Holograms have depth. Business cards that are holograms are definitely out of the ordinary. Imagine . . . 3-D without glasses. You can have a phrase like "See the depth of our business for yourself," or "Look beneath the surface." Krystal Holographics (365 North 600 West; Logan, UT 84321) can produce custom or stock holograms. They also have cards printed on crystals, glitter, or hyper-plaid background stock. You've got to see it to appreciate it.

These cards are definitely different, and how you use them should be different as well. Here's a case where you might want to have two sets of cards: a regular set that you hand out to almost everyone you meet, and the special customized holograms for specific customers. (Maybe customers you've already given the first card to, or someone who is definitely a serious customer or prospect.)

When you personally hand out a card that is a hologram, make sure you have something to say to call attention to the fact that it's a hologram and to make a bigger impact. Something like "Our company is more than what might appear on the surface. Check out our card."

OptiGraphics, 800-662-2813, converts 2-D to 3-D by layering multiple illustrations and photographic elements into a piece of

3-D "art" in the size of a business card. When the process is done, the 3-D perception produces a unique illusion. Definitely out of the ordinary.

Have a definite plan on how you want to use a card like this. These cards cost more, and you want to make an impact each time you give one out.

68

PLASTICS

Plastic Cards

Business cards made out of acrylic are definitely different. You can get cards made out of plastic that you can see right through. They're stiffer, stronger, and probably hold up better than business cards out of card stock. The only problem is you can't write on them. Customers can't put their own notes on them. They can't jot down prices on them. They can't put your cell phone, your home phone, and your Web site address on them. And you can't either. With the amount of phone numbers and technical information we have today, there always seems to be something else we'd like to add to our card. Sometimes we have to write it in. With a plastic card you can't. Unless you're giving out real credit cards (we should be so lucky), stick with something you can write on.

Nothing is worse than having a customer or client start to write down information about your business or service, only to find they can't write on the card, they don't have any paper, and you have to scramble around for a note pad. Make it easy. Skip the acrylic. Go with a card you can write on. It will save you time and eliminate headaches.

Bombardier Capital has a business card in bronze with nothing but their 800 number on it. It can be used as a file or refrigerator magnet. But it's not really a business card. It's a magnet, period. And it really can't be used for anything else.

69

THE SWEET TASTE OF SUCCESS

Candy Cards

Now here's a sweet idea: a business card made out of chocolate. Appeal to your customer's sweet tooth. It's a card they're sure not to throw away! In fact, they'll really "digest" your message. Obviously, chocolate business cards work best in cooler climates like New England, the Midwest, or the Northwest. In Phoenix or Miami, a melting chocolate business card would probably not leave the best impression on a prospect—it would be more likely to leave a stain on his or her suit. These are also not the kind of cards you want to carry around in your back pocket!

When giving out an edible card, make sure your recipient knows what it is. Tie it into your personality, or what your company does. ("We're a sweet company to deal with.") Don't just hand it out and leave it at that. Some of these edible business cards take a little explaining.

A number of companies make customized chocolate cards, and they're not as expensive as you might think. Your business card can be recreated in chocolate for about a dollar a piece. It's a tasty way to make your card stand out from all the others a prospect or customer has collected. Of course, once they eat it, your card is gone.

You can also have full-size chocolate bars wrapped with a label reproduction of your business card for around a dollar each, depending on the quantity you order. And the labels are big enough that you can put additional information on the backs: like your store locations, Web site information, and so on. Let's Wrap It Up, Inc. also offers custom-wrapped bite-size Kit Kat bars: a more traditional business card size, for seventy-five cents each. Customers can eat the candy and save the label as your business card. You could also give out the chocolate cards along with a regular business card: one for now and one for later. Or you can choose to follow up in the mail with a regular business card, maybe include a note saying something like: "You took a bite out of my card . . . now I'm hungry for your business."

There are other candy choices, as well. Sweet Impressions offers "candy calling cards"—small boxes

Companies That Can Make Chocolate Cards

Choco-Net: Customized chocolate business cards (logo bar).
Web site: www.choconet1.com

Let's Wrap It Up: Custom-wrapped Hershey's chocolate candy bars.
Web site: www.letswrapitup.com/business.html
phone: 248-360-2872
fax: 248- 681-9275

Nouveautés: Embossed and printed chocolate bars.
phone: 800-894-4438
fax: 201-890-0002

Sweet Impressions: Candy calling cards (small boxes of candy with space for a business card on top).
Web site: www.sweetimpressions.com/cards.html
phone: 800-323-8037

Wrappers-R-Us: Custom-wrapped chocolate bars.
Web site: www.wrappersrus.com
phone: 888-709-8818
fax: 602-248-0572

of four pieces of candy with a holder on the top for your business card. These start at thirty-seven cents each with a minimum order. Obviously, doing it yourself is an even more economical option. The staff at Fred Kiene & Son, Inc. in Grayslake, Illinois, have the words "Thanks! You're worth a mint to us" printed on the back of their business cards. They hand their cards out with a cellophane-wrapped peppermint.

All it takes to enjoy the sweet taste of success is a little creativity.

Now, having a candy card is one thing. Using it to your best advantage is another. It's a great way to establish rapport with receptionists. But upper management could take a dim view if you're expected to be very professional and use the utmost business decorum. Use some common sense. Candy cards have their place. You decide where that place should be.

70

CUTE . . . REAL CUTE

Cartoons, Drawings, and Illustrations

Cartoons and drawings have their place. Some are great. Some can be awful. You have to be careful with humor. It depends on the nature of your business and how casual you want your card to be. If you're going to have a cartoon, drawing, or caricature on your card, first of all make sure it is professionally done. Don't take that ten-dollar caricature of yourself that you had done at Disneyland and expect it to make an impression by having it on your business card.

If you've found a cartoon that specifically relates to your business or industry, and want to use it on the back of your card, remember, many of these are copyrighted. Nothing could be more embarrassing than handing your card to a potential client and having them remember the cartoon from a recent national or local publication. It's even worse if the cartoonist is someone they know.

If you're a veterinarian and want a cartoon of an apprehensive German Shepherd going in for a shot, you'll probably get a nice reaction with the cartoon on the back of your card. Particularly if the caption is something like "I might whimper, but I never cry at (clinic name)." Check who does cartoons in your area. It could be someone working for a local advertising agency, a sign painter, or a college student who does cartoons for a college publication. You also might think of contacting your local newspaper and asking who does the cartoon on the editorial page. They're often eager for extra work.

One thing about cartoons on business cards, or any line drawings that have a touch of cleverness . . . they get stale over a period of time. Do not use them for a long stretch. They're great for specific events, like Chamber of Commerce meetings, trade shows, consumer events, or any type of large meeting. But it can wear thin quickly, particularly if you're giving another card to the same person a few weeks later. That's where two sets of cards might come in handy . . . one with the cartoon or drawing, and one without.

You might find something that is cute or clever and want to put it on your business card. Here's a tip: Show it to five people first. Get their opinion. If only one or two start to show a smile, you may want to rethink putting it on your card. If all five think it's the greatest thing they've ever seen, rush to your printer. Don't waste another minute. Cute, clever cards can be tough to come by.

71

WHAT'S THAT NAME AGAIN?

Phonetic Spellings

When a name is hard to pronounce or read, phonetically spelling it out (in parenthesis) could be a face-saver for your customer. Your ethnic name might be easy for you, but for the person who gets your card it could be a bit of a problem.

For example: Shewczyk could be pronounced "Sheftic" in Polish or Ukrainian. You could write it phonetically, i.e. putting "Shef'tick" next to the name on the card. The last name Guillame (pronounced "Ghee'yom") could be written next to it on a card. Linda Koch from Orange, California, has "pronounced 'Coe' " written in italics next to her name on her card. She says that it saves time and aggravation for both her and the card recipient.

If you have an unusual first name, you could do the same. It will make your client more comfortable when he or she calls.

If your name is unusual or hard to pronounce, you might tell the person the correct pronunciation while handing them your card. Call attention to the fact that it might be hard to pronounce. Just because you've been using it all your life, doesn't mean it's easy for other people. Speak slowly. Let your name sink in. See if they repeat it. Once they say it and remember it, they probably won't forget you or your name.

72

KONICHI WAH

Foreign Languages

If you're doing business internationally, or if you'd like your clients to think you're involved with other cultures, here are some suggestions:

1. Rather than putting your name in Japanese, Chinese, Korean, or Russian underneath your name in English, keep one side English and the other side the language of the country you're doing business with. Show both sides when presenting your card. Call their attention to it.

2. Check for accuracy. Before having your cards printed, show them to someone who understands the language and see if it makes sense to them. Then double check it again with someone else who also understands the language and have them translate it back to you.

3. Does your mission statement, quotation, or company slogan translate well into the other language? Remember when GM introduced the Chevrolet Nova in Mexico, and then found out that the meaning of *no va* in Spanish is "Doesn't go." How does your card translate? Check it out before you have it printed.

4. You could have your title in a foreign language and the rest of your card in English. When you hand out your card to someone in the U.S., and your title is "El Grande Queso," you might get their attention by having them ask "what does that mean?" (Even if you're not the Big Cheese).

5. The American flag and the flag of the foreign country you might be doing business with is a nice touch. It shows togetherness. It's also colorful. Anything to make your business card stand out is a plus.

6. How about your mission statement in the language of the country you're doing business with? That could make a definite impact, just to let them know you've gone out of your way a little for them.

7. Now that you've got a bilingual card, how much of the language do you know? A few words? Learn something about the culture and the language, so when you give out the card you have something in mind you can respond with for instant rapport.

One of the easiest ways to get a quick start on the language is to go to one of the local bookstores and find a cassette tape or video series on learning the language for children. Don't laugh. It makes learning a lot easier, and you probably won't be able to converse overnight no matter what course you get. At least this way you'll know a few words.

8. "When in Rome, do as the Romans do." Learn the local customs when giving out a card. All countries are different.

Don't embarrass yourself. Access the Internet or go to your local library to learn something about business etiquette in the country you're visiting, or the do's and don'ts of conducting business with the person you're giving your card to. (For example, in Thailand it is considered very rude if the soles of your feet are pointed at someone—cross your legs carefully!)

9. If you're not sure of a particular word your recipient is saying, ask them to spell it. They might not know the correct pronunciation, but chances are, they'll know how to spell the word.

10. Go easy on the humor. Careful on the translations. Being "cool" to get a "rush" out of the person you're giving your card to may not go over well.

73

CRAYONS AND CALLIGRAPHY

All I Need to Know I Learned in Preschool

Subtlety, elegance, creativity, and cleverness can be accomplished with many different approaches on business cards. Liz Curtiss Higgs, from Louisville, Kentucky, is an author and speaker on "encouraging." Her cards look like someone did them with a crayon, but she had an agency design the card. They look great.

If you're a nursery school, day care center, sell kids toys, design children's clothing, having your card look like it's done in crayon can be really effective. The design has to be clever and clean and it shouldn't look like a four year old did it in five minutes. You can use stick figures, different colors, and childlike drawings. Think of the impact it could make on someone who is interested in what you do. If you run a nursery school and have a business card that shows you're child oriented, rather than giving a card that could pass for a Fortune 500 company, bet you get a better reaction and better results.

Toko-Yoko Gifts is a company that distributes Japanese products. They have their name done in brush strokes on the back of their card. It's done in Japanese calligraphy. Everyone wants to know what it says. It's a great conversation starter.

A calligraphy font is available through most print shops. Before you go and tell your printer you want to use it for your name or company name, check it out first. Some calligraphy is hard to read. Some Old English is also hard to read. If the name is very long, you might want to select a different font. When someone scans your business card, you've got about three seconds for them to absorb it all. Don't slow it down with a type font that needs a second glance.

74

X MARKS THE SPOT

Maps on Cards

If you're off the main highway, if you're so remote that your address is "go into town and ask somebody," you might want to consider a map to your place of business on the back of your business card. If people are continually calling for directions, or calling you to say they are lost, then a map should be more than a "maybe." It should be a "definitely."

There are some basics, if this is something you're going to do. Always indicate which way is North. A little arrow with an "N" could work if space is at a premium. Have at least three well known, easy-to-find starting points and landmarks. These could be a school, a hospital, a gas station, a post office, or any major building. Not everyone comes from the same direction. Have at least two major highways and four cross streets. Indicate where the traffic lights are. Make sure you show which side of the road your business is located on.

Something that works well on business cards is including the amount of time it will take to get to your business from a certain point. For example: "3 minutes from the turnoff on Highway 1," or "5 minutes from downtown Puckerbrush." This way, when they've driven 20 minutes, they know they have gone too far.

You don't have to be AAA or Rand McNally. Have the map drawn to scale, list area markings that are easy to find, and have landmarks inserted that everyone will know.

If your competitor has a map on the back of their cards, don't just copy their card and move the X. You might be saving a little time and money this way, but put more thought into it. Be creative and unique. Make it look like you're more professional than anyone else in your area.

75

HERE'S LOOKING AT YOU, KID

Mirrors on Cards

Here's an idea for a business card that is more than a business card. You can buy a small mirror in a plastic case through just about any premium catalog company. The case is just about the size of a standard business card, but slightly thicker. You can have your company name, your name, phone number, and anything else you feel is important on the front, and the back can have the words, "Take a look at our most important customer." Or "This is where our customer service starts." You get the idea. A mirror never seems to get thrown out. You know . . . seven years bad luck. It's amazing how people keep them in a desk drawer, a glove compartment, or a purse. And there it is in a sleeve that has your name and phone number, plus an address and company name.

The more you can have the sleeve or case the card goes in look like a business card, the better the chance of actually creating a business contact. You don't want it to look like just one more freebie, like a pen or a key chain with a company logo and phone number. One salesperson met a customer who he had given a business card/mirror to over forty years ago. It was even before area codes. The person still had it. They were still using it. Talk about longevity. And name recognition.

People love to look at themselves. Make it easy. There are any number of ways you can use mirrors along with business cards. If the mirror is unbreakable, you don't need the case. There are a number of plastic-based surfaces that can be made very reflective. These are great for people who like to look at their reflection every time they pick up a knife in a restaurant. Maybe the reflection from a plastic coating is more like you'd see in a funhouse, but it does get attention.

76

PENNSYLVANIA 6-5000

Updating Changes

Remember when phone numbers had a prefix with letters (GRanite, HOward, PEnnsylvania, ALpine, etc.?) You wouldn't think of giving out a card that old, but it's amazing how long some people will continue to use business cards with old or dated information. Check out the following:

1. Is your area code current? Telephone area codes seem to be changing by the week. You may have changed it on your letterhead, but are you thinking you want to use up your old business cards before you reprint with the new code? Don't wait. Don't cross out. Reprint your cards right away and throw out the old ones.

2. Do you have the right zip code? Do you have zip + 4? It gets mail to you faster, plus it looks like you're up to date.

3. Check your e-mail address. Take a look at your Web site domain name as it appears on your business card. Dots in the right place? Are spaces relevant? How about caps and lower case letters? Will your encryption work the way it's printed on your card?

4. If you have a suite or floor number, is it on the card? Is it correct?

5. Can people find you easily, once they come to the address on the card? Or should you be more explicit if it is in an industrial park or large office building?

6. Is your logo current?

7. Do you have an 800 number, or has it been changed to 888? Check it out.

8. Are the services you render the same, or should your card be updated?

9. Any new products not listed on your card?

10. Is your name spelled right?

77

I LOVE A MYSTERY

Clarity and Explanation

Maybe you just do business locally, in a small town. That's no reason not to put your area code on your business card. Business cards sometimes travel a long way. Statistics show that 20 percent of all business cards not only don't have the area code, but on those cards that do have the area code, it is wrong 10 percent of the time. Area codes change. Don't keep giving out cards with outdated information. Here are a few other things you may have forgotten to put on your card that your customer wants to know:

- A street address if mail goes to a post office box (many overnight services won't go to P.O. boxes).

- A little description of what your company does, if someone can't tell by the name. (The ABC Corp. could be anything from accordion manufacturing to drug smuggling.)

- Your name, not just your company name. Maybe you work for Amalgamated Pneumatic Pumps, but who are you? Make sure your name is on the card.

- An extension number next to your phone number if you have automated answering. (This will save time, irritation and aggravation.)

- Mr. or Ms. if your first name could be either male or female (Kim Slocum, Toni Hunt, and Rene Delaney are all male executives).

- ® or ™ if you use a registered trademark or copyrighted logo on your card.

- "USA" in the last line of your address if you do business internationally (Paris, Texas and Paris, France are quite a few miles apart). Make it easy for your recipient and the Post Office.

- An actual first name instead of just initials. (If you name is John, and everybody calls you JP, still put John on your cards. JP could go in parentheses.)

78

POP-UP POP-UPS

Pop-up Cards

Here are a few ideas for business cards that almost come to life. Bob Herlin and his company, Graphics3 in Jupiter, Florida, make pop-up Christmas cards, but they also make pop-up business cards on a limited basis. Imagine opening a two-fold business card and seeing a drawing table or airplane pop up from the middle. The ideas that you can have pop up out of your card are endless. If you'd like to get a sample of what this company can do for you, give them a call at 561-746-6746.

Another company is Perrygraf (19365 Business Center Dr. Northridge, CA 91324; 818-993-1000). These business cards in customized styles and shapes are not for everybody, but they do certainly make an impact by standing out from the rest.

Zeppelin DJ's in Guadalajara, Mexico, has a great card that is almost square (about 4 $\frac{1}{4}$ x 3 $\frac{3}{4}$) and is folded four different ways. Their printer came up with this original idea. When someone is handed the card, the folds start to unfold and it almost pops up in their hand. This business card also stands up on a table, and they use them to help promote their company at the parties they work. The card folds down to about 2 $\frac{1}{4}$ inches square. It really gets attention. You might want to check out unique folding patterns if you're interested in a card that is not flat all the time.

Cards with moving parts aren't cheap. But if you can increase your business with them, all of a sudden they become cost-effective. Check it out for yourself. This is one way to get a "jump up" against your competition.

79

DOUBLE DUTY

Cards That Serve a Practical Purpose: Magnets,
Slide Charts, Bookmarks

Maybe your business card could serve another purpose. It could double as a refrigerator magnet, a bookmark, a pre-paid phone card, or a reference card. It could be a map to a specific area or location. If most of your clients are overseas, you could put some of the basic American words and phrases on the back, something that they might use for reference. And those basic phrases could include slang or expressions we take for granted like: "cool," "up-to-speed," "right-on," etc.

If at all possible, give clients and prospects a reason to keep your card for a long time. Better still, give them a reason to keep it out in the open or at least take it out frequently.

A real estate agent keeps two sets of cards. To potential home-buyers, she gives a card with loan amortization tables printed on the back. To potential sellers, she gives cards imprinted with a helpful ten-step guide to selling a home.

One insurance agent gives cards that many have later found themselves grateful to have kept. On the back is printed a no-nonsense guide for what to do if you're involved in a car accident.

Some people choose to use their cards as a miniaturized catalog, highlighting their most popular items, complete with prices and order numbers.

Something else. You can have business cards made that are actually slide charts. You may have seen them: the ones that can transfer feet and inches into metric, generic names for prescription drugs, and mileage charts. The American Slide-Chart Corporation has hundreds, if not thousands of ideas. Write to them at P.O. Box 111; Wheaton, IL 60189; or call them at 630-665-3333.

Of course it doesn't have to be quite so practical. You can get just as much mileage out of having fun. A mobile disc jockey has a footprint guide to the "Electric Slide" printed on the back of his cards. Similarly, a dance studio has tango steps printed on the backs of theirs.

If you're still skeptical about incurring extra printing costs to have something printed on the back, consider this scenario. If you were ever caught without a piece of paper and needed some either to take down someone's number or give information, would you grab a stray business card someone had given you and scribble on the back? You just might. And the person who gave you that card has now become the person who provided you with scrap paper. Do you want to give out your business card or scrap paper? If you have interesting information printed on the back of your card, it will never become anyone's scratch pad.

FIRST A QUARTER, NOW A NICKEL

Leaving Room—Minimalism

You need blank space on your card. If you don't have blank space, it's going to look cluttered, busy, and boring. In the past, the suggestion was to be able to put a quarter somewhere on your business card where no letters were covered up. Things change. More information is being passed around today. Maybe you no longer can fit a quarter on your card, but at least have some white space the size of a nickel.

If you have very little white space on the front, don't make the mistake of cluttering the back. You won't be able to tell back from front. If you use both sides, leave room to be able to put two quarters on the back without covering up letters.

What can you cut out on the front, to leave space for that nickel? Can you use more abbreviations? Take out some numbers? Put the Web site on the back? Smaller logo? Different font? Smaller type size? Scrap the mission statement? Less product information?

Your business card is a reflection of your business. You don't want it to look like a junk yard. You want it to be a little tidier than that. And you want enough blank space for a coin to fit without covering up letters.

DON'T BE A VICTIM OF HYPE

Avoiding Exaggeration and Falsification

I received a business card the other day from a company that bills itself as "America's #1 Health Food Source." They have no store or office. They work out of their garage and stock minimum inventory. Not quite what their card depicts.

Obviously you want to have an elegant, professional, creative, clever, memorable business card. But don't use hype, statements you can't prove, or misleading information. Don't use them, that is, if you want referrals, new business, or repeat business. The same is true with bland, mundane, trite phrases that everybody else uses. They make your company look boring. And anything misleading will only come back to haunt you.

For example:

• World's greatest . . .

• The biggest . . .

• The King of . . .

• The area's only . . . (when other companies are similar)

• We're number one

- Drive a little, save a lot

- Satisfaction guaranteed

- Where the customer is king

- We aim to please

- We stress quality

- We sell for less

- We discount

These phrases don't stand out. Hundreds of thousands of companies have the same words on their business cards. Get your brain in gear and start thinking about what you can put on your card that nobody else can copy, or nobody else has already used. And then check the words you're using when you're handing out your card.

Be different. Be creative. Be unique.

You also don't want to put in any guarantees you can't back up, or anything else that could be construed as simply hype. Today's public, meaning the buyers, consumers, and individuals you come in contact with, are educated. They can see through false promises and overblown advertising. Choose your descriptive words and phrases very carefully.

82

BORN IN THE USA

Drawing on National Pride

If your product is made in America or you promote your business as "Made in the USA," bold red, white, and blue colors do stand out. The American flag as a background can work. One American manufacturing company has a verse of "America the Beautiful" on the back of their card. You can have a quote from Lincoln or Washington. You can have a picture of the Statue of Liberty, Mount Rushmore, or the White House.

Other graphics or pictures that convey the American-made image are the flag, eagle, Uncle Sam, the Statue of Liberty, the White House, the Liberty Bell, the U.S. Capitol building, or a montage of many of these things on the back of your card.

If letting your customers or clients know your product is made in America is important to you, the words can go under your corporate logo or somewhere else on your card. You can also put a small graphic of the American flag somewhere on your card.

83

EVERYBODY LOVES A WINNER

Awards and Accomplishments

Have you won a Grammy, Emmy, trophy, or some local distinguished award? Maybe it should go on your card. If you've won "Contractor of the Year," it could be printed on your card. Or maybe it's a charitable accomplishment, "Employer of the Year" designation, or something of local significance.

If you've completed a course that gives you a certificate of accomplishment in your field, it could be listed on your business card. Many schools not only grant degrees but also offer specialized certificates. Magic words to use on your card could include:

- Certified

- Licensed

- Authorized

- Registered

- Professional

- Member of . . .

You can also build your own credibility with phrases like:

- Inventor of . . .

- Founder of . . .

- xx years of experience

- As seen on . . .

- honors, medals, degrees, certificates, and titles you've been awarded

You don't need to load every achievement, honor, or major accomplishment onto your card. Be selective. In most cases, state only the highest or most important designation or degree.

If you're going to put letters after your name, be clear about what they stand for, or they will fail to have a tangible image or mental association. Even if the acronym is well known, like CPA, you could still be in "Cleaning, Pressing, and Alterations." Make it clear if it's on your card.

84

BULLETS AND BORDERS

A Little Creativity Goes a Long Way

Two design elements you can use to dress up your business card and emphasize important points are bullets and borders. Bullets are small icons that are placed in front of points that you want to draw attention to. On the front of your card, you may want to use bullets to highlight the lines you carry, the services you offer, or the benefits of doing business with you. Bullets help you break up a block of text and make it easier to read and more visually appealing.

For example, here's a list in paragraph form:

We carry a full assortment of Yamaha, Roland, Korg, Baldwin, and Samick instruments.

Here it is in bullet form:

We carry a full assortment of instruments from:

• Yamaha

• Roland

• Korg

• Baldwin

• Samick

If you have a long list that you would like to include on your business card, consider printing it using bullets on the reverse side of your card.

Another point to consider is that bullets don't have to be round. Think about using a small icon that relates to your business. For example, I recently received a brochure from the Disney Institute at Walt Disney World which used small Mickey Mouse ears icons as bullets. Be creative! Other icons to consider include: flowers, four-leaf clovers, musical notes, hearts, footballs, diamonds, tires . . . anything that fits your business.

Borders can really spice up a card. You can do something as simple as a thick line paired with a thin line all the way around the card or something as fancy as a Celtic knot design encircling the card. The border can help carry out a card's theme. For example, a cowboy or a tack shop might have business cards with a border in the shape of a rope. A florist might encircle her business card with flowers.

A border doesn't have to go all the way around your card, either. It can run at the top and bottom or on the two sides. You may use it only at the top to anchor the card or you may use a simple border to highlight an important part of the card. It's up to you.

85

LEATHER AND METAL
AND EVERTHING ELSE

Your Card Doesn't Have to Be Paper

That company that makes the ringing telephone card also makes blinking cards. You can call Clegg Industries at 310-225-3800 and they can put you in touch with a distributor in your area who can produce a business card with a blinking light that operates on a very tiny, self-contained battery. Perfect for those late-night meetings or dark conference rooms.

If leather is your thing, contact Torel (P.O. Box 592, Yoakum, TX 77995; 512-293-2341). These leather business cards can be printed and embossed in one or two colors. But remember, they are hard to write on.

How about Braille? Makes a great second set, conversation starter, and shows a humanistic endeavor. You can put Braille impressions on your existing printed cards or have them made from scratch. Contact Access USA (P.O. Drawer 160, 242 James St., Clayton, NY 13624; 800-263-2750).

Other stocks you might not have considered could be:

• photographic paper

• wallpaper

- sheet metal

- parchment

- wooden strips or veneer

- thin metal

- cloth that is paper backed

- sand paper

- rubber

- or any papers that match an individual's business materials: ledger paper, graph paper, blueprint paper, prescription pads, etc.

Whatever stock you choose, make sure you can duplicate it in the future for additional runs. Trying an unusual stock can have striking effects.

86

SNIFF HERE

Scratch 'n' Sniff Cards

Scratch 'n' sniffs and scents are in magazines, store invoices, in packaging, and advertising. You know which magazines are going to smell good. It's easy to do this on business cards. This is definitely not for everybody, but it sure gets noticed. Ask your local printer about scented inks or you can do it yourself.

If you're a floral shop, lingerie store, perfume and cosmetic boutique, or any kind of business that lends itself to this type of thing, just a drop of perfume or scented oil on a few cards at a time can do the trick. The danger is having too much on one card. This is one case where less is more.

You can also use those sprays you find in car washes and auto shops. The ones that feature lemon, spice, vanilla, new-car smell, etc. This is something you can have fun with. If your last name is Rose, you can have a card that smells like a rose. Iris McNeil is a floral designer in Manhattan. Her cards always smell like a flower bouquet.

Careful who you give these cards to. You don't want an allergic reaction, or an upset wife who might think her husband was fooling around, only to find he picked up a business card from a department store's cosmetic counter on the way home, while shopping for an anniversary gift.

87

BIG, BIGGER, BIGGEST

Oversized Cards

If you're into oversized business cards, there are a lot of ways to make them more effective. There is no law that says business cards have to be business card size. And with the amount of information some people are trying to cram onto them, bigger can sometimes be better.

One very clever idea is to have a business card with a reverse side lined like a legal pad. In fact, it could have the same proportions as a legal pad. Since it would be slightly larger than an average-sized business card, it would stand out when put together with other cards. And since the back is lined like a legal pad, there is space to write notes, ideas, and information when handing out your business card.

If your business card is the size of an index card, you might be able to actually mail it without an envelope, if it meets postal regulations . . . another plus. Also, if your card is 3 x 5 to simulate the size of an index card, having it lined like an index card might be a nice touch. That way writing on it might seem like the most appropriate thing to do.

It's amazing how many people put notes on business cards after they receive them. And how many people make notes on their business cards as they hand them out. Make sure there's enough space to do this. Oversized business cards could be the answer.

A perfect example is American Red Ball World Wide Movers in Seattle, Washington. Their business card is normal size but it is ten times as thick. It's actually a little notepad with a spiral bind. All the company info is on the front, the first page is a calendar (probably for planning your move) and about a dozen pages for notes. Nice.

Marty Tinianow at American Consolidated Entertainment Service in Denver, Colorado, uses the acronym A.C.E.S. for his company name. His business card is (guess what) an ace of hearts playing card with address, phone number, etc. on it. It's larger than a regular business card, it stands out, and people don't misplace it, or throw it out as readily. He can fan out three or four at a time, and then use his thumb to push one ahead of the others when giving it to a client or customer.

There is no such thing as a "regular sized" business card anymore. So, what size? What works? How about postcard sized?

If you go directly to using a postcard, you can still use it for a business card. It's one way to stand out, and they are inexpensive and easy to print in full color. Also, you've got plenty of space for all kinds of information, and they're perfect for a quick personal note. A bunch of them might be tough to carry in your pocket or purse, but the advantages could outweigh the disadvantages, depending on your business.

Here are more of the advantages:

• There is room for all the relevant data like product information and additional store/branch locations.

• Oversized cards are more likely to be noticed and talked about.

• They can also serve as a small brochure.

• Oversized cards have more design options.

• Your card will stand out from other cards.

• There is plenty of room to write.

• Oversized cards can be easily personalized.

If you're going to carry these cards around with you, put them into an envelope first, before trying to stick them in your pocket or purse. They will get easily bent because of their size. Be selective when giving them out. In an office setting they're great. Handing out an oversized card outside your place of business might force your recipient to fold your card in half just to put it in their pocket. Think about which route you want to go and how you're going to use an oversized card.

88

WHICH TYPE IS RIGHT FOR YOU?

Different Fonts and Type Sizes

The words on your business card convey more than just your name, your phone number, and what you do. Type styles are extremely expressive; the font you choose is just as important as the graphics or colors that you choose. Make selections that suit the function, the mission, and the message of your company.

One of your primary concerns should be readability. Your card is like a tiny billboard—but the operative word is "tiny." Certain fonts look great on a regular page but end up looking like a messy blur on a business card. The lower case letters of certain typefaces work poorly in small sizes. Tiny spaces in letters like *e* and *g* tend to bleed onto themselves, turning the letters into illegible blobs. The same can be a problem with numbers. Do you want to lose a prospective client because she thought that the last digit of your telephone number was an 8 instead of a 6?

On the subject of readability, don't use more than two different type styles on one card because it tends to be too distracting for the eye. Also save reverse type (light colored words on a darker background) for use as an added touch.

Practice "word economy." Of course you want to include as much information as possible, but it's wise to be choosy. Elements in larger type will be seen as more important, but you don't want any of your precious information to be overshadowed. You don't want to have so many words on your card that the font would need to be read with a magnifying glass.

Don't be afraid of decorative fonts. Used correctly, they can pack a lot of impact into a very small space. The key is to match the personality of the font to the personality of your business. Pretty script with swirls and flourishes is fine, but may be inappropriate for a funeral director or an investment counselor. Conversely, stiff or formal fonts might not be the best choice for a wedding consultant or a florist.

See what happens when you put aside your preconceived notions about lettering. Explore your options; consider the non-traditional. Who says you have to capitalize the first letter of every proper noun? Who says you have to capitalize anything at all? Try using all upper case or all lower case lettering. Or mix it up for emphasis: brINKman publications.

Spacing is another place where you should feel free to break the rules. Extended spacing can add a fresh look to certain elements. Stretching out a name or an address line can be visually interesting and can open up the area it's in, making it appear less crowded. Additional spacing can be used for emphasis as well: L i g h t Works Studios.

Be aware of which typefaces go together and which do not. If you're not feeling confident making lettering decisions, don't be afraid to seek the advice of a professional designer. What you don't want is for your card to look unprofessional or thrown-together.

89

GREEN MEANS GO

Color Choices and Combinations

Take a look around you. Stop and notice the colors in your surroundings and how each one makes you feel. Now look at the papers on your desk: the mail you received today and maybe even the pile of business cards you may have collected in your own drawer. Pick up a few and look at the colors in each one. Are there any that you gravitate to? Why? You probably can't even explain it. Few people can, but that doesn't stop them from making split-second decisions based purely on the colors in their line of vision.

Color isn't just there to look pretty. It should be going to work for you, reinforcing your message, and telling people what you do. Using color can draw attention to particular elements and it can captivate the eye of the beholder. It can help you organize your information. The use of color also conveys added professionalism—some are apt to judge the success of your business by how much you can afford to spend on your business cards.

Color is a universal language. Colors convey nonverbal information and strike people on an almost purely emotional basis. Grays and browns are viewed as steadfast and conservative and might not work so well for creative occupations such as artists or designers. Oranges and sunny yellows are fun and carefree—terrific for a travel agent but deadly for an accountant. Pastels are perfect for a stroller manufacturer, but not quite suited to an auto body shop.

Take care with traditional associations. Red and green together, for instance, are so deeply enmeshed with Christmas that it might be difficult to disentangle them. Red and white stripes bring to mind barber poles and candy canes, black and white stripes still bring to mind old-fashioned prison uniforms.

While there are traditional associations you may want to avoid, there are others you don't want to alter. For the same reasons that adults often look puzzled when children color skies green and grass pink, objects that appear contrary to people's expectations negatively affect their sensibilities. We think of zebras as black and white, not green and white. Unless your company name is Green Zebra Music, Ltd., or something of that nature—better to stick with black and white.

Try adopting a signature color. It helps you build your company's brand identity. Could you ever imagine the McDonald's arches in any other shade of gold than the one they use? Much in the way that companies develop logos and use them on every sign and piece of printed material, some also choose a specific, numbered Pantone® shade to unify their image.

Something else: Take care to consider clarity and legibility. Traditional black on white is as clear as you'll find, but that doesn't mean it's your only option. In most cases, sticking with light-colored stock is your best bet for legibility. Even with light stock, it may be wise to make colored type larger to ensure the most clarity. It's possible to use colored stock, but the wrong combinations will make your message suffer. White text on black is the toughest combination to pull off and you can't write on it. And most colors on blue don't fare well either. Always keep in mind that the color of the stock underneath will alter the color of the printing. Adjust for stock differences: that perfect shade of green will look different on yellow stock than it will on white.

If you're serious about designing your business cards, no doubt you've already begun to consider your color options. What color for the lettering? What color for the graphics? Even if you opt for pure black ink, you might be considering paper stocks of a shade other than white . . . there are thousands of them. With so many options, how do you choose? The bottom line is this: knowledge is power. Talk to people, visit some printers. Learn as much as you can and make informed color choices. Capture the power of the spectrum and put it to work on your business card.

90

HOLD ME, FOLD ME

Folding Your Business Card

If you're willing to spend a little more to stand out from the crowd, try breaking the mold. Folds and unusual shapes have worked successfully for a variety of businesses.

Most business cards are a standard size and shape. They are aligned either horizontally or vertically. Creativity has altered the playing field—and in some cases broadened it quite a bit.

The change in size of your card doesn't have to be to uniform; you can change only the length or only the width.

If you're ready to start "thinking outside the box," literally, you may also be ready to consider the limitless possibilities of die-cutting. The die-cutting process can take you anywhere from minor alterations (like a corner cut off, a simulated bite mark, or a half-star cut into an edge) to a shape completely unique to your business (an aluminum can for a beverage distributorship or a dog bone for a pet supply company). While a die-cut card can be the ultimate "standout," keep in mind that you'll have to budget the cost of having dies made. Also be careful with your choice of materials, as some don't tend to cut crisply. Ask your printer for suggestions and advice.

And then, consider using a fold. Many companies that feel oversizing or novel cuts would be too "over-the-top" for their market have chosen to add a fold (or even two) instead. Folds give your message more breathing room while still maintaining a standard shape.

- Top- and side-fold cards can either be the same size on both halves, or can be made as a short fold, with the top half cut to any length you choose.

- A gatefold opens in the center, like a tiny set of double doors. Much as one would when opening a gift, the recipient holds his or her breath for a split second before opening the folds, awaiting the "surprise" it contains. Whatever you print inside, that card is going to be remembered for quite some time.

- Accordion-folds can give you more space than you can even fill, but be careful not end up with a card that's too bulky to be easily handled.

- A specialty version of a folded card is the mini-book. These can consist of several "pages," giving room for an extensive amount of information. The open edges can be cut as miniature folder tabs, as graduating short-fold cuts, or however you decide. These are especially good for use as a mini-brochure or mini-catalog.

Specialty folds and sizes aren't for everyone. They won't necessarily fit neatly into your business card holder or the recipient's card filing system. Because of their uniqueness, they may be set aside from other contact information, allowing for the possibility of being forgotten. And they can be expensive to produce. But they're at least worth taking the time to consider if your budget allows and your company's personality is right for them.

91

CHECK OUT THE COMPETITION

Taking Cues from Other Business Cards

Take a look at your competition, who else is in your line of work, and then look at their business cards. What can you do that's different? What can you do with your business cards that they should be doing but aren't?

Here's an idea. Go to your competitors, or send someone else. Get their cards. Then go to some surrounding businesses that aren't competitors and get their cards as well. Go home, and spread them all out on your kitchen table. Which ones get your immediate attention? Which ones are dull and boring? Which ideas can you blend into your cards?

That's step one. Next call every advertising agency, from the yellow pages in your phone book. Talk to one of the account executives. Ask them to send you their card. They will. They love to do it. They're supposed to be good at design. Check out how their business cards look.

The next step is to call every Mobile DJ in the phone book and ask for their brochure and a card. These are the people who spin CDs and entertain at weddings, parties, bar mitzvahs, class reunions, and the like. Mobile DJs actually have the very best business cards, because they don't advertise much on TV or radio, they're not in the newspaper, and most of the bookings come from word of mouth and business cards. Many of them are really terrific.

Now, go back to your kitchen table. Spread everything all out again. What catches your eye? How does your card compare now? Pick the best five. What are the best points of each, and what can you utilize from them to make your card better?

Don't rely on one person to give you all the advice on designing your card. Check out the competition. How do their cards look? How do they use them? Talk to them. Have other people you might know get some input. You never know where the next business card idea is coming from, and it might be your competition, the business down the street, or someone in another category all together. Keep your eyes and ears open.

THE INTERNET AND BUSINESS CARDS

Web Addresses

If you have a Web site, you want the domain name on your cards. Trouble is, you've already got enough information on your card to fill a small book. Sometimes a Web site address can take the place of a lot of printed information. You can write, "Check all other additional information on our Web site at www. _____" or "Additional phone numbers at www. _____" or "A complete list of _____ is on our Web site, find us at www. _____."

One of the best ideas is to simply list your Web site on the back of your card, which gives room for someone else to write as well.

When you see a proof of your business card, pull up your Web site using the address listed on the card to make sure it is correct. Nothing would be worse than a misplaced dot or space. Your customer or client may assume other information on the card is also wrong. Make sure there are no mistakes.

Web cards (800-352-2333) can make up a business card/postcard that looks like the front page of your Web site complete with buttons, pictures, and graphics. You can have three- or four-color on the front and black-and-white on the back. They have some very clever ideas to entice customers to visit your Web site. There's even room to address and mail them.

FEEL ME, I'M EMBOSSED

Embossing

Raised letters. Do you need them? Do they fit your business? Years ago raised printing was the sign of an elegant, expensive card. That's when most cards had a company, a person's name and title, and an address and phone number. Nothing more. Today, with the amount of information most cards contain, embossed cards could look out of date, or could be artistically unattractive.

How about reverse embossed? That's where the name of your company is indented onto your card. Everything else is regular print. And if you like special print effects, you could consider metallic inks. These inks come in hundreds of colors, including silver and gold. They are high density and can be used to print over other inks and colors. Metallic inks work best on coated stock and can look very rich.

Fluorescent inks don't look as rich, but they are truly eye-catching. They reflect light very well. If you're a neon or lighting company, this could work. Ask a printer for samples.

Maybe you could just have your logo embossed on your card, if you think embossing is important. Get somebody else's opinion before you decide.

SIGNS OF THE TIMES

Look at Billboards for Inspiration

Your business cards are really pocket billboards. Some of the best ideas for layout and design are also found in magazine ads and on highway billboards. Take a look around. What gets your attention? Your brain is exposed to over 1,500 advertising hits a day . . . and that's without turning on your TV or radio.

As you're driving down the highway take a look at those billboards. Particularly the ones from national companies. You'll notice they work their magic in seven words or less. Very few of the good ones have more than seven words. So when you're thinking of a new idea for your business card and looking to upgrade it into something that's more dramatic, here's a place to start. Billboards only command a second of attention. You need the right picture, the right artwork, and definitely the most memorable message in as few words as possible.

Your business card is not going to say "next exit," so disregard those billboards. And forget about the ones that suggest "so many miles ahead," or "ahead on the left." However, the ones that really grab your attention and express their message in a split second can offer you some ideas. What grabbed your eye? Can it work on a business card? You actually have more room on a business card than on a huge billboard because a person holds a business card in their hand for a longer period of time.

On a well-designed business card you want your entire message to immediately create a good impression when first scanned. Choose your words carefully.

95

THE BEST OF THE BEST

The Best Cards to Go to for Examples

Here are some of the professions and industries that have the best business cards and what makes them good.

1. Mobile DJs. The people who spin CDs for weddings, private parties, and special events have some of the best business cards. This is their best source of advertising, since you seldom see them on TV or in the newspaper. They're clever and creative, five-color, have interesting folds, and are unique.

2. Advertising agencies. This is how they earn their living. Check out their cards. They're paid to be creative.

3. Sign painters. You'll usually see more than a splash of color from some of the larger companies. Their business cards are a link to their talent.

4. Entertainers. Comics have funny cards. Musicians have cool cards. How can you adapt their style into your business card?

5. Artists. Most artists have an elegant, simple card, depending on their style of art. Every once in awhile you'll find a business card that really stands out. Can they paint one for you?

6. Photographers. Many times a sample of their work appears on their card. Maybe even a self portrait. See how the photo-professionals do it.

7. Graphics illustrators and design companies. These people usually come up with pretty good cards since they work with graphics and computers all day. Maybe they can do one for you very cost-effectively. Get some samples of what they have already done.

8. Printers. Ask them who they have done business cards for. They should be able to show you dozens and dozens of samples. What do you think of their work? Would their ideas work for you?

9. Major automobile dealerships. These people spend a huge amount of money on advertising. Many times they show it in their cards. Take a test-drive. Ask for a card.

10. Radio and TV stations. They want to make an impression. They are also in the entertainment business. They try to out-do each other with better business cards. With twenty or more stations in most markets, you should be able to see some real creativity by asking them to send you an account executive's card.

Using Mobile DJs as good business card examples, check out Andy Austin's card. He's a mobile DJ and owner of Sight and Sound DJ's in Richardson, Texas. His phone number is 972-742-3869. Ask him if he'll send you one of his cards. He paid $5,000 to have the name of his company drawn artistically to be reproduced on the front of his cards. That's right. Five thousand bucks! Van Gogh and Rembrandt would be proud. It's very abstract. It's in five-color. His name, address, phone number, etc. is all on the back, and the back is in black and white. He had it commissioned to be painted by Dallas artist Sasso. Sasso is very well known nationally, and is a highly respected artist in Texas. When Andy gives out a card he tells everybody how much he paid to have SIGHT AND SOUND DJ'S painted by Sasso for his card. It's a great conversation starter. Many people ask for two.

He finds that people hang on to his card and show it all over the place. And what usually comes out of their mouth is "You know, he paid Sasso $5,000 to paint the front of his card!" Maybe you have a well-known artist in your town.

Music Manufacturing Services in Toronto has a business card that looks like a CD or a CD-ROM, but it's clear plastic. It's obvious that it can't be played, so it won't hurt a computer or CD player. But it sure is unusual. It fits in a pocket, it can fly like a Frisbee, it can handle very large type, and it can contain lots of print information. Can a miniature version of your product be used as a business card?

John Jerit, owner and president of American Paper Optics wanted to make sure that his company's business card would be a "keeper," one that people would hold on to and remember. John pioneered the combination business card/3-D eyeglasses. Traditional contact information is printed on one side of each card/pair of eyeglasses, and the other side advertises the different kinds of glasses his company produces. Maybe they're a little expensive, but they certainly are creative, clever, and memorable.

Design Infinity, a graphics company in Toronto, Canada, has a card that's reverse embossed, with text front and back. It is clever and effective. On the front they list all their phone numbers and Web/e-mail information in a small indented space that you have to turn the card to see. Their phone number is 416-513-0841. Ask them to send you a card. It might give you some ideas to take your card to another level.

96

IN CONCLUSION

Things You May Not Have Considered

Okay, your head is spinning and you've looked at enough business cards and business card ideas to make you dizzy. Don't stop there. After you've collected your competition's cards, business cards from outside of your industry, and sample cards from just about anyone you meet, take out a pad and jot down not only which ones stand out, but what parts of each card are really noticeable. List what makes them different. Think of how you can use some of the ideas to improve your card, and then how you can make it even better. Here are ten things you may not have considered:

1. Your corporate logo in color, with everything else in black and white

2. Your signature in place of your name

3. Lots of color

4. A clever fold

5. An undersized or oversized card

6. A unique cut

7. A customized font

8. A picture or photo that takes the place of many words

9. An interactive card that blinks, rings, or changes color when held

10. A card that looks like something other than a business card

You want a business card that reflects you, and even makes you look better than you are. You want to give it out with pride, and you want to give to the right people.

So how do you stack up? What can you do differently to increase your business starting tomorrow, when those words "Here's my card" come out of your mouth? With a great business card, some selling smarts, and a good personality, the sky's the limit. Oh, by the way, you have to give it a shot. Good ideas are not enough. You have to implement them. You won't know what works until you give it a try!

97

POSTSCRIPT

You'll Never Believe This One

There are some real master networkers in the world today. Some excel to the point that they are in a league of their own. The ones who come to mind that I have exchanged business cards with are Dick Clark, Harvey MacKay (author of *Swim with the Sharks Without Getting Eaten Alive*), Lou Holtz (former Notre Dame football coach), and Muhammad Ali. I also had an opportunity to give President Clinton a card. Bill Clinton is one of the best networkers the world has ever known. I met President Clinton at a fundraiser for Hillary while she was campaigning for Senate in upstate New York. At this little gathering I had a chance to give Bill a video for aspiring musicians that we had just produced entitled "How to Find Gigs That Pay Big Bucks." In four seconds of face time he told me "It was cool," asked, "who was it intended for?" and said, "I can use this when I'm out of office," then disappeared into the crowd. He thought the video was clever and showed it to a lot of people. As he was leaving he said (to no one in particular) that he wondered who did the video.

Fighting my way to get near him to give him my card, I found a dozen autograph seekers who looked like they were playing in the backfield for the Minnesota Vikings. It was tough getting close. I thrust my card at him, he took it, signed somebody's business card, and then autographed my business card and gave it back to me! I said, "Hey, what's this . . . I gave you my card so you'd know who did the video." He said, "Do you have another?" Of course I did. I'd be too embarrassed to write this book if I didn't. And now I have one with President Clinton's name written over mine. I show it to everybody. Here's a guy who knows how to schmooze. I'm glad I had enough business cards with me that day. Never leave home without them.

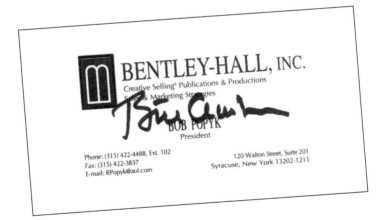

ABOUT THE AUTHOR

Bob Popyk is president of Bentley-Hall, Inc., with offices in Syracuse, New York, a company specializing in sales and marketing strategies. He is also a columnist for many national trade and business magazines including the *Business Journal, Kitchen & Bath Design News, Swimming Pool/Spa Age,* and *Music Trades*
Magazine. He is a frequent television and radio talk show guest, and publisher of the *Creative Selling®* newsletter, which has subscribers all over the world.

Bob works with many national retail and wholesale associations and is one of today's most requested keynote speakers on networking, sales, and customer retention. He has also produced a number of books and industry-specific publications and videos that are distributed worldwide.